Colin Huycroft.

7.6.73.

DOROTHY RICHARDSON
THE GENIUS THEY FORGOT

Also by John Rosenberg

Novels

The Savages
The Double Darkness
Mirror and Knife
A Company of Strangers
The Desperate Art

Dorothy Richardson and her husband in the garden of their friend Peggy Kirkaldy in Essex, in the early 1930s.

DOROTHY RICHARDSON
THE GENIUS THEY FORGOT

a critical biography

by

JOHN ROSENBERG

DUCKWORTH

First published in 1973 by
Gerald Duckworth and Company Limited
The Old Piano Factory
43 Gloucester Crescent, London NWI

ISBN 0 7156 0655 7

Printed in Great Britain by
Ebenezer Baylis and Son Limited
The Trinity Press, Worcester, and London

To the memory of Rose Odle
with affection and gratitude for the help
that made this work possible

CONTENTS

CONTENTS

Preface

Dorothy Richardson's place in the history of the novel, as the creator of the 'stream of consciousness' method (a phrase which she detested), and as the immediate precursor of the Joyce of *Ulysses*, Virginia Woolf and Katherine Mansfield, has become obscured, for reasons which will emerge in this work. The fault may partly have been her own; in that she guarded her privacy so carefully throughout her lifetime, that at one period, when she was famous, various odd legends about her were current, some even affirming that she was a man who wrote in the guise of a woman. Whenever she was approached for biographical material, she supplied the most allusive and evasive accounts of herself; and once, asked for her photograph, to be printed with an article, she sent a snapshot of a baby.

In fact, her life was a full and complex one. There is a key to part of it in *Pilgrimage*, her sequence of thirteen novels, which were largely autobiographical, but covered a period corresponding to only a quarter of her lifetime. On her death in 1957, there survived as biographical material, apart from *Pilgrimage*, a few brief and for the most part imprecise articles, some unpublished notes of her own, chiefly to do with her method of writing, and about six hundred letters to and from various friends, relations and associates. The letters, collected and collated with tireless dedication by her Literary Executor, Rose Odle, seemingly added little to the known facts, scant though these were. There were also a few surviving friends who could give first-hand accounts of her. But once again these accounts were sketchy. Even these friends had known her only partially and for limited periods.

However, my closer study of the letters yielded many isolated details or allusions which could gradually be sifted, juxtaposed and pieced together into an accurate account of Dorothy Richardson's life and the evolution of her work. At this point, such information as was available from her friends was useful in linking and verifying some of the evidence. I must acknowledge my debt to Mr. David Grad; to Mr. Philip Batchelor, Dorothy Richardson's nephew; and to Mr. P. Beaumont ('Owen') Wadsworth; as well as a far greater one to Mrs. Rose Odle, who died on 30 October 1972, and to whom this work is dedicated. I am also indebted to Messrs. J. M. Dent for permission to quote considerably from their Collected Edition of *Pilgrimage*; and to Messrs. Knopf for these quotations from their American edition. My wife Elizabeth has helped me with her critical and editorial advice, and with her understanding of the subject. Mr. Francis Odle kindly allowed me to use, for the frontispiece and jacket, two photographs in his possession.

In 1961, an American scholar, Dr. Gloria Glikin, interviewed Dorothy Richardson's only surviving sister, Mrs. Jessie Hale, who died in the following year. An article by Dr. Glikin, published in 1963, contained therefore several useful points of information which are duly acknowledged in the References to Sources, at the end of this work. Another American scholar, Professor Joseph Prescott, published in 1959 'Seven Letters from Dorothy Richardson', received from her when he wrote for information for his *Encyclopaedia Britannica* article on her. But the letters to Professor Prescott, most of them mere notes, were scarcely more informative than previous articles.

These, then, are the main sources; together with *Pilgrimage* itself, and the body of essays, sketches, stories, reviews and poems by Dorothy Richardson which were published in various periodicals. Professor Prescott compiled in 1958 'A Preliminary Checklist of the Periodical Publications of Dorothy M. Richardson', lacking at that time the details of her articles in *The Dental Record*. Quotations in the text of this book are mainly from her own letters or works, and are all identified in the References to Sources.

Since *Pilgrimage* is closely autobiographical, as Dorothy Richardson herself confirmed from time to time, and since it was her life's work as well, I devote several chapters to setting out briefly the main characters, incidents and issues of *Pilgrimage*, so that these may be related to the actual events and people of her life. I also offer a critical summary of her work—its aim and its achievement—towards the end of the book. In this Preface, therefore, I make no general statement or judgment, preferring to let her life and the examples of her work reveal her.

Dorothy Richardson, who changed the course of the modern novel, only to become one of the great unread, was born in the country town of Abingdon in Berkshire on 17 May 1873. She was the third of four daughters of Charles Richardson, a tradesman who aspired to become a gentleman: an ambition that was to prove disastrous for his family.

The Richardsons, of pious and prosperous Wesleyan stock, had been settled for several generations in Berkshire: in Abingdon and also in Blewbury facing that part of the Downs where Alfred the Great had led his army along the Roman Road, and where earlier still the Celts were supposed to have conducted their sun-worship on 'Blewburton', a strange escarpment of plateaux rising one above another in this bleak stretch of countryside, its line of bare hills broken by few trees.

There was an increasing Wesleyan population in this area; and the Richardsons, 'stern puritans', were of a character that matched the harsh landscape. A portrait survives of each of Charles's parents. These are formal portraits; and Thomas and Mary Richardson are dressed in silks and lace befitting the status of a successful master grocer and his wife. The faces are firm and severe, both handsome in their tight-lipped way. These good looks Thomas passed on to his son Charles, but not, it transpired, his business acumen. Charles had other interests.

Following the publication in 1859 of Darwin's *Origin of Species*, and the controversy that it set off, science was beginning to emerge as nothing less than a new religion. Darwin's theory of evolution, by disallowing the notion of divine guidance or pattern, struck at the basis of theology. Young Charles Richardson, living only seven miles from Oxford, had university friends and, reading Darwin, he was totally converted to his theories. Charles was no doubt present at the Oxford debate of 1860, when Thomas Huxley, Darwin's supporter, who was to go much farther than Darwin himself in opposing orthodox beliefs, refuted Bishop Wilberforce.

Charles became a member of the British Association for the Advancement of Science, the society, founded in 1831, that brought laymen and scientists together in research and study. In addition to his scientific pursuits, Charles had begun to cultivate the tastes and manners of a gentleman. Tall, fair-haired and personable, he fitted his new rôle quite well. But as the Richardsons' only son, he was tied to the grocery trade—at least for the present—and he must bear the slights connected with his status. Then and long afterwards, this was a society in which a tradesman's customers ignored him if they happened to pass in the street.

The first suggestion of something better was the marriage of his sister Elizabeth in 1861 to a man called Henry French. French was no grand connexion, an assistant mathematics master at the Wesleyan College in Trull Road, Taunton, Somerset. But at least his profession enabled him to style himself a gentleman. The magic word had entered the Richardson family tree.

To Somerset, clearly a good hunting-ground, Charles followed his sister. In the village of East Coker* lived a family called Taylor. These were people as different from his own as was this lush countryside from the bleak Berkshire downs. Traditionally 'gentleman farmers' and Anglicans too, which was socially better than the 'chapel' Wesleyans, the Taylors were cheerful extroverts, more emotional and unstable than the Richardsons but amusing and attractive with their 'perpetual but haunted cheerfulness'. Edward Taylor, the father of this branch of the family, was a manufacturer of canvas for sailing boats; but he still qualified to have his name listed among the gentry in the local directories.

His daughter Mary was small, pretty, bright and gay,

* The *East Coker* of T. S. Eliot's poem, of his ancestors, and of his burial place.

2

and she was dazzled by the tall, handsome Charles Richardson with his assurance and his clever pronouncements. Despite his scientific bias, he was quite prepared to marry her in her own parish church of St. Michael's in East Coker. Charles Richardson and Mary Miller Taylor were married on 18 July 1866.

Settling into a pleasant house in Marcham Road, Abingdon, they worshipped henceforth at the Anglican church of St. Helen's, near where the quiet river Ock flows into the Thames. By his marriage, Charles had been enabled to leave the faith of his family, if not their trade. But his present house, situated between the two branches of the Richardson business, one in Ock Street and the other in the suburb of Marcham, was socially not good enough. The fashionable place to live in Abingdon was Albert Park on the northern outskirts, consisting of some fifteen acres of parkland which had been presented to the town by the governors of Christ's Hospital charity in 1864.

In 1867 Mary had her first child, a sturdy blonde daughter, Frances Kate. Charles had wanted a son, but it was early days yet. Apart from her domestic ties, Mary was somewhat isolated in Abingdon. Her husband's family—his parents in Abingdon and uncles, aunts and cousins in Blewbury—were a joyless lot after the exuberant country life of her own family in Somerset. The Blewbury Richardsons—Uncle William, a grocer, draper and baker, Aunt Caroline Stone, cousin Susan Jane, William's daughter, proprietress of a school—the women with their 'chapel hair, parted and shined back into a little ball'—were of the same severe character as Charles's parents. Nor was Mary's relationship with Charles one of equals : she was naturally bright, but she did not share his intellectual interests.

A second daughter, Alice Mary, was born towards the end of 1868. Four years later, Mary again became pregnant. Charles's longing for a son—to be called after himself, and to follow in his footsteps as a rationalist and a gentleman—had become more pressing. This time it must be a boy. In this same year he moved his family into a large house in Albert Park : another ambition fulfilled.

On 17 May 1873, Mary was delivered of another sturdy, fair-haired infant, a girl. They christened her Dorothy Miller. In childhood—after the birth of the fourth and final child, again a daughter, Jessie—Dorothy, who had so disappointed her father by being born a girl, was sometimes referred to by him as his son, and called 'Charles'; and of all the daughters she was the least domesticated, the one least encouraged in feminine ways.

On 13 January 1874, when Dorothy was not yet a year old, Charles's father died, leaving an estate of something under £8,000 together with properties in Abingdon, Blewbury and Bicester. The bulk of the estate, apart from certain charges and legacies—mainly a life income to Charles's mother and a substantial bequest to his sister—went to Charles. And it was enough to set him free of the trade which he loathed.

Disposing of the business, he increased his staff of 'devoted old-fashioned' servants at Albert Park. It was a spacious house set in large gardens. He aimed to live as a gentleman of leisure, 'an amateur of most of the arts and a deeply interested spectator of the doings of science'. He invested most of his money speculatively. Safer investments were not for him: he needed more income than he had, to keep up these standards and devote himself to scientific research. In 1869 he had become a life member of the British Association, 'never missing a gathering, at home or abroad'.

Dorothy's first seven years were idyllic enough, in this pleasant, cultivated, affluent background, with the downs and woods and the beloved large garden to play in. Her earliest recollection was of this garden, of tottering down a path between banks of massed flowers with the bees humming among them. The blaze of colours, the dazzle of light and sound, so profoundly affected 'this small being to whom they first, and they alone, brought the sense of existing', that she would often refer to this scene in her writing. Already she was keenly aware of impressions of light, of landscape and of different qualities of sound. She had 'noted the play of light through a wood, had visited a hill-

4

top and discovered that the world went on beyond it, had noted . . . the flow of that river, on and on, away, homeless and free'. 'The existence, anywhere, of anything at all' seemed to her childish mind astonishing.

At five she was sent for a year to a small private school, at which point she shed 'a quite dreadful little name : "Tottie !", and willingly learned to read, fascinated by the variety of combinations of letters and fired by the challenging irregularities of our unphonetic English spelling'. Words and their rhythms fascinated her ; another memory of these days was 'the sound of a voice reading *Hiawatha*' to her, its vivid rhythms lulling her 'into forgetfulness of the fever of chickenpox'.

The atmosphere at home began to be uneasy. Charles was having money anxieties. He knew that he was living beyond his means, but he was Micawberishly sure that things would work themselves out. He was more concerned with enforcing his ideas on health and diet, and he now 'refused to eat baked meats and had everything roasted on a spit or a roasting jack'. But while he had a share of the Richardson toughness and singlemindedness, Mary was more vulnerable. She began to suffer from headaches and depression, and she laughed less often.

The four girls had very different temperaments. Kate, the eldest, sturdy and sensible in character and looks, but always 'indulgent' of Dorothy's 'escapades and wickedness', was almost wholly a Richardson ; Alice, delicate and nervous, was very much a Taylor. The two younger girls were a mixture of both sides. Dorothy, physically like the Richardsons, derived her sensitivity from the Taylors. Charles, for all his intellect and interest in the arts, was a man of no great awareness or perception. He reacted strongly against unconventional ideas or attitudes ; as when a few years later, finding on the library-table of his club a copy of the not very avant-garde periodical *The Review of Reviews*, 'that world-shaking venture . . . was by him lifted, with the tongs, and placed upon the fire'. His wife's troubled state of mind was evidently beyond his understanding.

Disappointed though he was that she had borne him no

B

son, he had other aspirations. Having attained Albert Park, he set his sights on London. There, nothing and no one could associate him with Richardson the grocer, and he would be near to his club and to the British Association headquarters.

But when in 1880 he told his family that they would be moving from Abingdon, it was not to London that they went. His investments had depreciated. He must retrench and live cheaply in the south coast town of Worthing. He could make the excuse that the seaside air would be good for the girls and Mary.

Dorothy, attached to her home and to the surrounding country, was bitterly unhappy at leaving Abingdon. By comparison with the Albert Park mansion, the house in Worthing, 6 Victoria Road, was a cramped little villa, an 'unhomely home' without character, without their own familiar furniture and without a proper garden. Even the younger girls were now aware of their straitened circumstances, which restricted their activities and made their mother from now on 'a semi-invalid', and brought them 'the dawning, amazing realisation of illiberality, in thought and feeling, hitherto absent' from their lives.

Dorothy and Jessie, with only eighteen months between them, were close friends and played happily together, but always under the shadow of the family trouble. The Richardsons had always been musical, but music was now 'almost absent' from their home. Worthing itself, with its built-up town, seemed a tame, dull seaside compared with the wilder Devon coast at Dawlish where the family had spent earlier holidays. This was 'only the channel sea, in place of the boundless Atlantic'. Even the church here, and its ugly name, St. Botolph's, depressed Dorothy after the perpendicular Gothic church of St. Helen in Abingdon, which had offered 'in every direction an eyeful of beauty'. She grew to hate the drive to St. Botolph's, down a bleak succession of mean, treeless roads. 'St. Botolph's,' she wrote in after years, 'at the age of six . . . saw my first spiritual desolation'; and 'the local school made no impression' on her.

6

In 1883, when Dorothy was ten, Charles suddenly had a stroke of good fortune. His investments had improved. At last he could move his family to London, or just outside it, to the pleasant well-to-do suburb of Barnes with its large houses set in extensive grounds.

From the moment the Richardsons 'turned in, from a wide roadway lined with pollarded limes and drove up the approach' to the new house, 4 Northumberland Avenue, 'between may trees in bloom, and swept round past a lawn surrounded by every kind of flowering shrub, to pull up in front of the deep porch of a friendly-faced, many-windowed house', life seemed very much better. Soon they began to join in the genteel round of suburban pleasures : the tennis-club, the supper parties, the private dances and the boating. For the moment Charles had money enough for quite lavish entertaining, and he took on a governess for the younger girls.

But the shadow on their lives still persisted. It must have maddened Charles, who forgot his troubles so readily, to find that his wife, in these opulent new surroundings, was still nervously unwell and that his daughters were not quite at ease. Dorothy was especially difficult, and she sometimes 'scared and alienated' all her family 'by some apparently unprovoked outburst of wrath and resentment'. What they lacked was self-confidence. They couldn't altogether believe in their prosperous new life, after the ups and downs of the past years, and all the 'intermittent distresses' over their mother.

Dorothy, 'wilful and quite unmanageable', seemed very sure of herself, and yet she suffered acutely from shyness, feeling 'rightly shut out' from other, happier people. Her parents and elder sisters found her hard to control, as, by her own account, she 'flouted their authority' and chose to 'despise their wisdom'. The governess, teaching 'the minimum of knowledge and a smattering of various "accomplishments" '—and trying vainly to bribe her with chocolate mice to stop her from slipping under the table whenever she was bored—was 'torment unmitigated, apart from music lessons', and left after a year.

7

Dorothy and Jessie had their own separate nursery world, and their own secret plans and ideas ; and only Jessie 'ever presumed to criticize' Dorothy. One evening they decided to run away together to the gypsies, who encamped from time to time on Barnes Common. In the kitchen yard there was a small brick shed housing three built-in bins, one for ash, one for cinders, and one for kitchen waste. These bins, huge as cauldrons, fascinated the girls. They planned to hide here and slip away after dark.

In fact they got away without hiding in the bins. They took with them 'a basket full of nursery odds and ends to sell' to the gypsies. It was dusk, and the lane to the common was deeply overshadowed by trees. The silence and the shadows began to alarm the two children. Halfway to the common, they panicked and turned back. Their parents had missed them by now, and were white-faced with concern ; but, tolerant 'almost to excess', they sent the girls to bed without so much as a scolding.

Charles's tolerance was more tried by Dorothy when she began to disagree with his beliefs and to dispute his '"rational" approach to reality'. People at a British Association meeting, she would later describe as having 'a kind of deadness that was quite unlike the deadness of the worldly people . . . They were almost something tremendous, but not quite'. She wrote of 'the dark veil under which I grew up. Darwin fecit'. She and her father were, by one account, 'too much alike' and therefore they 'clashed'; although he recognized her intelligence, taking her 'to concerts and lectures'. He sent her to Southborough House, a remarkable school at 17 Putney Hill, a few doors above The Pines, 11 Putney Hill, where for seven years the poet Swinburne had been living in the care of his devoted friend Watts-Dunton.

In the previous decade, liberal education for girls had made great advances, but there was still much opposition to it. The tradition persisted that girls should be taught domestic skills and accomplishments—and that indeed they were by nature fitted for nothing more. It was a widely-held theory that physiologically women's brains were inferior to men's, that in the chain of development women were, genetically, lesser beings than men. This was used as justification of the social injustice that deprived educated women of the vote; and only since the Married Women's Property Act of 1870 had they any rights over their own property.

Even in the arts, it was argued, women had contributed little, compared with men. Dorothy could see the obvious fallacy in this argument. Denied education, tied to a domestic round that often included annual childbearing, how could women be judged by their achievements?

Miss Harriet R. Sandell, headmistress of Southborough House, was a disciple of Ruskin and believed in the most liberal kind of education, encouraging her girls to think for themselves and take sides on current issues. In English lessons there was for Dorothy 'the fascination of words, of their sturdy roots, of the pouring in from every quarter of the globe of alien words assimilated and modified to the rhythm of our own speech, enriching its poetry'. Miss Sandell even instituted a sixth-form class in logic and psychology. Dorothy attended the class, but 'psychology . . . with its confidence and its amazing claims, aroused, from the first, uneasy scepticism'. She rose to be head of the school, and grew so attached to it that 'leaving school, in spite of all that lay ahead, was tragedy'. She made one lasting friend among her classmates, a girl called Amy Catherine Robbins.

Amy was bright and sophisticated, with a scientific mind. She was planning to take a degree in mathematics. Her assurance made Dorothy feel awkward and naive, on their walks to school together along the Upper Richmond Road, then just beginning to change from its village character to a drab suburban high street. Amy, with her scientific cleverness and confidence, seemed bound to achieve a brilliant place in the world. Dorothy, in contrast, never knew what to say to people. Social life sometimes seemed unbearable in all its artifice : she could 'never belong to that world'; and at times she longed to get away from all these 'refeened, gloved, urbane, nice gentlewomen'.

She was growing into quite a pretty girl, of middling height, with long thick fair hair and a very fair complexion, her prettiness only marred by the glasses that soon she had to wear.

She cared passionately about injustice and stupidity—the injustice, for example, that she saw in her home relegating her mother to an inferior position, when to Dorothy it seemed that her mother had far more real intelligence and awareness of life than her father, with what she described as the typical 'man's patronizing illusions' about women. She looked on her mother as a 'saint', who had taught her to 'see life as jollity, and unconsciously fostered . . . deep-rooted suspicion of "facts" and ordered knowledge'.

Dorothy was young and susceptible, and one side of her nature wanted very much to belong to the pleasant social world around her. For a time she got over her feelings that she was an outsider. There were attentive young men, 'to be in love was . . . fatally easy', and one of these young men seemed serious about her.

She began to think of marrying him, and spending the rest of her life in this Barnes world of comfortable houses and servants and music and social life. The Richardsons had their own 'sunk lawn for tennis, regulation size, beautifully chalked by the gardener'; and at sixteen Dorothy became the youngest member of the tennis club, and 'with the help of a handicap of fifteen . . . and of the next youngest member, a lad of eighteen, who volleyed everything from the net', she won several tournaments. Kate was even more spectacular. In the middle of a most dramatic match, her bustle burst, and 'there shot out on to the lawn the little cushion inside it covered in red turkey twill'.

Of these ladylike clothes, Dorothy wrote humorously: 'Not only did we play tennis and rounders in these perilous garments. We also sculled and rowed and punted in them, to say nothing of skating, and later, cycling in them. And cycling it was that brought the first breath of release by substituting, for ONE of our petticoats, KNICKERS, but only for the brazen few. Not much, it was thought, to choose between them and the utterly abandoned females who, chiefly in America, sported bloomers. Not long, then, before "divided skirts" came coyly to the rescue.'

Dorothy was also a clever actress, her ear for nuances of speech and sound making her an excellent mimic, as there was 'not on earth a speech sound' she could not imitate. She played the piano well, and she thought of becoming a musician or an actress.

At home there were regular musical evenings. 'The scores of Gilbert and Sullivan, and other musical comedies, eagerly purchased after visits to the theatre, also dance music and popular songs, were relegated to the schoolroom piano', to make way for the classical chamber music that Charles preferred. He himself played the violin. There were dances too in the large drawing-room. All these pleasures sometimes outweighed her 'longing to escape from the world of women' and discover a freer kind of life. She even enjoyed 'the awful deadness of the English Sunday' for a sense of stillness that it gave her. The local Church of All Saints, she liked especially for 'the music of its services, music, ruled by a master and confined to the work of masters, that caught and for years trained and disciplined my young senses unawares'. But she found herself 'chafing . . . under the average sermon'.

At a garden party she attended, there was a palmist telling fortunes. Dorothy entered the booth and was told that she would marry late in life, and would live to be old. Then the fortune-teller asked if she had done any writing. 'No,' said Dorothy; whereupon the woman said gravely, 'Start now'.

At this moment when it seemed that the idyll of life in Barnes 'was to go on for ever', there came a sudden warning. Charles said they must economize and entertain less. It was nothing to worry about, he assured them. But some of the servants had to go, and the girls must make do with their last season's dresses.

However, appearances were to be kept up. Charles maintained his own standards : the club and the British Association, his 'excellent cellar' from which on dinner party days he could be seen 'climbing upstairs tenderly carrying cobwebby bottles the maids were not allowed to touch', and afterwards there was always the ritual of 'the sacred bottle of green chartreuse warming itself on the pale-blue-tiled hearth in front of the polished brass bars of the drawing-room fire'.

But soon there were no dinner parties at all, and the girls were required to help in the house. This pleased Kate, who was 'willing ... to explore the unknown mysteries of domesticity'; but Dorothy, that 'Charles' who was known to be helpless in the kitchen and at housework, was spared by the older girls.

Then for a time things improved. Charles's stocks had gone up, and they entertained again; but the old dread still troubled them all, particularly Mary, whose headaches and nervousness increased. Charles was still resilient, in spite of 'disastrous speculation'.

Even in the next year, 1890, he was still confident, when he had to tell Mary that they 'were poor'. The rest of his family knew that 'there was no hope of redemption'. After all 'the ageing, deadening shifts they had invented to tide them over humiliating situations', they would be exposed as the criminals they were, offenders against the great Victorian cult of prosperity; and this time their disgrace would be complete. Bankruptcy in the 1890s was a stain impossible to expunge.

Nothing was yet certain. The last stages of his ruin were protracted. For Dorothy this time 'seemed the end of life'. Her suitor had moved off, and nothing was left for her at home. She wished to get away, but also to be of some help to her family. 'Since in those days teaching was the only profession open to penniless gentlewomen', she decided to look for a post as a governess or teacher, if possible abroad. As a child, she had been on a brief family holiday to Belgium. Her impressions still remained of that holiday, and the excitement of a new, different, more vivid world with a 'something we do not possess, a certain kind of happiness'.

She went secretly to a West End scholastic agency, was interviewed and took the first post that she was offered: as a pupil-teacher at a finishing school in Hanover. Her family were 'horrified' at 'this outrageous enterprise', but as usual Dorothy got her own way.

On a wintry day early in 1891, she said goodbye to her tearful mother and sisters, and, it seemed, to the whole of her childhood. She was going in search of her 'real self', after all the years of overlaying her identity with the conventions and patterns imposed by Victorian family life. She was armed with a stiff sense of duty and honour, and a sometimes painful truthfulness, with a concern for 'the problems of free will', with all her inexperienced intelligence and ardour, and with a trunk full of clothes that were now, since the family reverses, out of fashion and shabby.

Charles travelled with her, on the Channel steamer and on the train across Holland and Lower Saxony, to put her into Fräulein Lily Pabst's hands in Hanover. For a picture of Fräulein Pabst and her school, we have to turn to *Pilgrimage*, where Dorothy portrayed her as a powerful, moody character. These German finishing schools were hotbeds of emotionality, and Fräulein herself was given to outbursts of temperament and sentiment.

Dorothy's extremely English reserve, and her liking for solitude, were out of place in such a school, and made her once more an outsider. She longed to be able to relax and be more like other people. Hanover itself, as she later, nostalgically described it, was 'beautiful, with distant country through the *saal* windows, its colours misty in the sunlight; the beautiful, happy town and the woodland villages so near'. She was fascinated by the narrow mediaeval streets of Hanover's old quarter, and by the strangeness of the Gothic or Breughel-like faces, especially of peasants in the countryside. Through her keen perception and her 'faculty of wonder', she had moments of sudden and 'almost insupportable happiness'. But it was always with people that her difficulty lay ; she could 'rarely communicate with people at all, right away' : she lacked 'the technique' ; and the world of inanimate things was a refuge for her. She believed that she had let down her family, because of this inadequacy. In escaping to Germany, away from 'the devils of family contacts', she had been thinking of herself more than them. She had accepted the post simply because she 'liked the idea of going abroad'. She was making her own life away from their trouble and her mother's nervous illness.

A letter from home brought the news that her mother's condition had worsened. Her father's affairs were still unsettled, and Mary was being worn down by the uncertainty. On the brighter side, Kate and Jessie had both met men who wished to marry them, in spite of the family disgrace, and Alice had found a post as governess with well-to-do people in Wiltshire.

Dorothy was at once relieved to be going back to England, and ashamed at her relief. It seemed such a waste of her six months in Germany that she had never quite joined in the life of the school. After all, she had loved Germany and, as she later described it, 'the music and the words and the happiness of the German girls'. She had been alive here as never before, without knowing it, mostly taken up with her failures, and now it was too late to change.

She would have to try to find out where she belonged. The time in Germany, despite her mixed feelings about it as a 'brief and fascinating and horrible experience', had made her more than ever determined to carry on her search. She felt a great eagerness to be even more independent, convinced as she was 'that many of the evils besetting the world originated in the [Victorian] home and in the institutions preparing women for such homes'. She was back in England, at home, with troubles closing round her, and her mother, it seemed, was near to breaking down completely. But still, with her unswerving 'tenacity of purpose', she held on to this sense of adventure, of her 'life opening out' before her.

With Kate and Jessie both engaged, Mary rallied a little, and Dorothy could again look out for a post—but in London this time, to be near at hand whenever she was needed.

The Misses Ayre's school in Alexandra Villas, by Finsbury Park in North London, seemed a remote place to Dorothy, but she liked the letter from the eldest Miss Ayre, written in a clear fine hand, that 'subtly . . . drew me towards her', as she recalled in later years. North London itself seemed dreary and depressing. In *Pilgrimage* she describes it as 'ugly and shabby'. This first journey in the omnibus to Finsbury Park took her through a long succession of bleak streets, enlivened only by garish shopfronts and signs, with scarcely any greenery. But Miss Ayre was as attractive as her handwriting ; middle-aged, elegant, kindly and vague. Dorothy agreed to take the post, in spite of the drabness of the neighbourhood. This school, this 'backwater', would at least be a refuge to see her through the worst of the troubles at home.

It soon appeared that she had a vocation for teaching ; she taught the child rather than the subject, and that made her pupils alert and alive to their lessons. As she had believed since the days of her early disputes with her father, that awareness and perception were far more important than facts, she could teach them 'the difference between knowledge and knowing'. She made one lifelong friend among her pupils at Miss Ayre's, the girl whom in *Pilgrimage* she calls 'Grace Broom'.

Almost from the start, it was clear that Dorothy couldn't stay long at Finsbury Park. The work was too easy, and she was no further on in her search for an identity and a place in the world. In her hours of freedom she would walk endlessly in the rather tame expanses of the park, with its shrubberies, boating lake and playing grounds laid out in primmest Victorian fashion, a landscape as static and dull as her life here.

One pleasure she learned during her time at Miss Ayre's was a love of bus journeys in London. The long bus ride home would take her through many different districts of London. Gradually she came to be familiar with them all, and to feel that in the centre of London, with its beauty and poverty and ugliness and all its variety of peoples, on this 'pavement of heaven', as she called it, there was something more attractive and alive for her than personal contacts.

Charles's struggles to retrieve his lost fortunes dragged on into 1893, when he was finally made a bankrupt. The

15

house and most of the family possessions were sold. The Richardsons were helped by Kate's fiancé, John Arthur Batchelor, a steady kindly man some twelve years older than Kate, who insisted on giving up to his future parents-in-law his own house at 15 Burnaby Gardens in Chiswick, across the Thames. Though he worked as an agent for a company manufacturing thread and tapes for bookbinding, his great passion was music. On Sundays he played the organ in the Church of St. Anne and St. Agnes in Gresham Street in the City of London, and it was the musical tastes of the Richardsons, those evenings of private recitals at Northumberland Avenue, that had first drawn him to them.

Batchelor's kindness eased the final disaster of the bankruptcy and sale, but it couldn't stop Mary's deep depression, or Dorothy's feeling of guilty shame. In April 1895 Kate married Batchelor at the same City church where he was sometimes organist. From their honeymoon at St. Mawes they came back to a house at 6 The Avenue, only a few streets away from his former home where his parents-in-law were now living.

The second family wedding, Jessie's to Robert Thomas Hale, known as 'Jack', took place in June. Hale was a pleasant young man, and Dorothy liked him; but the marriage of the sister who had always been closest to her, with whom she had shared a separate childhood world of private allusions, left her even more alone.

At Jessie's wedding the best man, Fred Fenton, 'a dark intense creature who was heading for the Cowley Fathers', attached himself to Dorothy, talking very seriously of literature and religion. Despite his vocation, he was evidently attracted to Dorothy, but he was too earnest for her. He tried again a few years later when she was working in Harley Street, but she gave him no encouragement when he came to see her there; and a third time, decades afterwards, when he was a widower, he turned up yet again.

By 1895 she had moved on from Finsbury Park to a post in the country near London as governess to the two children, a girl and a boy, of Horace Avory, Q.C., a brilliant criminal lawyer who subsequently became a judge. Avory was a 'cold, controlled advocate', later famous for his dispassionate summings up and for his 'unnervingly silent manner on the bench'. His intellect was like her father's, factual and impersonal—the sort that always drew her fire.

With Alice farther away in Wiltshire with her employers, the Harrises, a family who had made a fortune in the bacon-curing business, and with Kate and Jessie married, it fell mainly on Dorothy to look after her mother. But she found it more and more difficult to make contact with Mary. The doctors suggested that Dorothy should take her away for a holiday in Hastings. The change and sea air might do her good. So to Hastings they went in the autumn of 1895.

Dutifully Mary let herself be taken for walks on the sea front, or along past the ruins of the Conqueror's castle; or sitting on the Pier, she would dully watch some performance in the pavilion. Hastings was very like Worthing, farther west on this Sussex coast—not a happy memory for them.

Mary would sometimes seem better, but only temporarily. So the days passed, in the closeness of their mean genteel lodgings where nothing untoward must be seen or heard to happen. At night Mary lay awake, ill and tormented in her mind. Dorothy, tending her, felt trapped and helpless; but by a friend's account, she 'devoted herself' to her mother, and 'it was humanly impossible for a young girl to do more than she had done'.

On 29 November Dorothy went out for an hour while her mother stayed behind to rest. The weather was unsettled and oppressive. *The Times* noted that this was 'the tenth consecutive day on which the sunshine recorder . . . gave a report of "none" for the sunshine of the day. The period has been marked by incessant gloom during the daytime . . . The humid air has . . . made anything like steady work almost unbearable'. Dorothy returned, from her walk in this miserable day, to a room dim and silent. There was blood on the floor where her mother lay dead, her throat cut with a kitchen knife.

The Coroner's Inquest brought in a verdict of suicide. The funeral took place in London. For Dorothy the death

17

of her mother left an awful silence. She 'felt not only loss, but failure'.

Charles was given a home by the Batchelors, though intermittently he lived in genteel poverty in lodgings. In 1904, when the Batchelors moved to Long Ditton, he joined them in their house in Cholmley Villas. It had a garden to the Thames, where the Batchelors kept a skiff and a punt. But Charles had always been a walker, and crossing by the ferry near the end of their road, he could walk along the towpath for miles, sometimes to the east towards Barnes. Except for the two years at Worthing, he had spent all his life by the Thames: first at Abingdon, then at Barnes, and now at Long Ditton. In these last years of his life, he still kept up his scientific interests, and helped his young grandson with homework in these subjects.

The Hales were less settled. After the birth of their daughter Nathalie, they took a house in Hastings and ran it as a boarding house. But it was an uncertain, seasonal venture. They thought they might emigrate. Alice seemed permanently settled with the Harrises in Calne, a pleasant village in Wiltshire.

Dorothy alone was unaccounted for. She could have found another post as a governess, or gone into a school; the Ayres would have welcomed her. But that would have been a step backward. She had no money, was unqualified for anything but teaching, and the death of her mother had left her feeling numbed. There was no consolation for her in religion: she had not the 'docility, fear, blind obedience' that she thought it exacted.

London drew her, with its 'power . . . to obliterate personal affairs'. The centre of London at least offered cover: she could be what she liked, or be nothing, in all that anonymous throng.

Harry Badcock, christened John Henry, had been born in
Barnet in Hertfordshire in 1864; but his roots, like
Dorothy's, were in Berkshire; and some of his relations
lived in Abingdon and had been friends of the Richardsons.
Another John Badcock had been Thomas Richardson's
trusted clerk in the grocery business; and if he were also a
relative of Harry Badcock, then it was an ironic reversal that
Dorothy was now taking a post as Badcock's secretary-assis-
tant in his fashionable dental practice at 140 Harley Street.
Badcock's partners were a father and son, the Peyton Balys.
They and he were also neighbours in West Hampstead;
they all got on well, like one big family, and this comfortable
atmosphere pervaded the surgery.

Dorothy, starting work there in 1896, had a hard, exact-
ing job, with long hours. Her duties included preparing the
alum and other materials, keeping the instruments ordered
and sterile, getting in supplies, arranging and despatching
repairs, and sometimes even delivering them 'by hand on
my way home'. She also kept the appointment book and
detailed accounts, and acted as receptionist-nurse in the
surgery, as she gradually acquired the necessary skills, and
the tact to soothe nervous or imperious patients. She was
continually up and down the stairs, and working in rooms
that were 'either overheated or draughty'. Her salary, £1
per week, was raised after a few months to £1. 5s., as the
partners were pleased with her work.

They 'insisted on her wearing black . . . little cheap black
frocks with lace collars'. This suited her fair hair and complexion, but she had grown very thin and she sometimes
looked excessively pale against the black dresses. She was
trying to put aside money, 'by a cheaper way of living', to
help her family. Lectures and concerts, though most of
them were free, sometimes cost her a fare. So she was

half-starved, eating only snacks at an A.B.C. or Express Dairy or 'Dutch Oven of blessed memory'. She liked these unpretentious cafés, in the West End or Bloomsbury or down towards the City. Among the shabby anonymous people who frequented these places, she felt safe from 'the dread claims of relatives and friends'. She was learning 'what London can mean as a companion'.

She tried to avoid close involvements with people, her only friends being two girls who shared a Bloomsbury flat, where she spent long 'evenings of intensive talk'. One of the girls was a German, Ellie Schleussner, 'from a Prussian officer sort of family', who had translated several plays by Strindberg. Dorothy and Ellie used to go together to St. John's Westminster, where the liberal young preacher, Basil Wilberforce, famous for his good looks and his cats, pleased his feminist hearers by describing God as 'the father-mother spirit of the universe', and by praising 'the divine curiosity of Eve'.

Slowly, Dorothy was beginning to make her way in London. She moved into Bloomsbury, to a room in its north-eastern, shabbiest district, where its succession of squares had their boundary at the 'narrow, crowded, disreputable lane of the Euston Road, still, at that date, remembered by the elderly as the hunting-ground of garrotters'.

At 7 Endsleigh Street, in a terrace of crumbling but still-handsome Georgian houses, grey-stone and pilastered, 'thick-walled, spacious', with rooms of good proportions, fine staircases, ornamental plasterwork and pedimented doorways, and dusty but tree-filled gardens at the back—a kind-hearted widow named Mrs. Keziah Baker kept a lodging house. Dorothy's room was at the top of the house, in an attic set back behind a parapet and facing west. Sitting at her small table in the window alcove, which caught the late evening sun, she had a view of the trees of Tavistock Square to the left and those of Endsleigh Gardens to the right.

Her room was grimy and meanly furnished, but she felt at home in the shabby old house. Apart from the Bakers, it was inhabited by a floating population of tenants of many nationalities and classes : students, waiters, doctors, people down on their luck; a cross-section of the district. They came and went anonymously; there was no one to involve her, and her 'London life was sacred and secret, away from everything else in the world'; for 'there lay upon the oasis to the north of the British Museum a peace deeper than any to be found elsewhere in London proper . . . to emerge from one quiet square was to find oneself almost immediately in another, with peace intact . . . no hint of distant, tumultuous thoroughfares'.

To the British Museum she found her way, securing a Reading Room ticket. The circular room, with its row of desks under the great grey-glass dome, became a second home to her. She later wrote of it that 'some of the happiest days of my life were spent there. If I were offered five minutes in London, it is there they would be spent'. Here she read philosophical, political and scientific works. For a time these intellectual interests took the place of any personal involvement. She was trying to find a way of thought, or belief, that could hold her. Years later, re-reading a book that had impressed her at that time, she was 'instantly . . . back in my freezing attic, ill-fed and worse clothed, solemnly remarking, in a letter, that the only thing I really cared about was the dawn, in my mind, of a new idea !'

London at this time was a melting-pot of ideas, philosophies and religions. It was the age of the suffragette movement, of the gathering power of socialism and anarchism, of great and gifted cranks, of vegetarians and Quakers, of revolutionaries and cabbalists. All these worlds Dorothy Richardson set out to explore : 'fascinating secret societies to each of which in turn I wished to belong and yet was held back, returning to solitude and to nowhere, where alone I could be everywhere at once, hearing all the voices in chorus.'

Socialism in England had found a characteristically moderate form in the Fabian philosophy preached by Shaw and the Webbs, both to the converted and to young aspirants like Dorothy at the Fabian Nursery, where Socialists under thirty, some in their early teens, attended discussions and lectures.

All her youthful reforming spirit was fired by these

movements and causes; and yet, for all their humanitarian basis, she mostly found them lacking in common humanity. The Fabians with their noble principles, their handwoven garments and their vegetarian diets, seemed to her too rarified, and disconnected from everyday realities. She would write of them that they 'were a league to arrest cruelties. But a cold, cynical, jesting league, cold and hard as thought, cynical as paganism and cultivating a wit that left mankind small and bleak, in a darkness where there was no hope but in intelligent scheming. Even the women . . . were all either as hopelessly logical as men, or methodically pink. And the men; the everlasting prize-fight, the perfect unsociability underlying their cold ideas. Except for one or two. And they were idealists, blind with the illusion that humanity moves with one accord.'

The Anarchists—believing in the natural goodness of man and his ability to live without governments, prisons or police, all of which institutions they would replace by a network of mutual, personal agreements—seemed nearer to man's individual needs, if somewhat impractical.

The academic world also seemed to her divorced from reality. Her cousin, C. M. French, the son of Elizabeth and Henry French, the schoolmaster of Taunton, was now a mathematics don at Cambridge; and she sometimes spent week-ends with him and his wife, and met 'their blinkered, comfort-loving, academic friends'. The Frenches were very kind people, and he was a cultivated man (in a way that was rather too conscious for Dorothy); but in the academic atmosphere, sedate, inturned and parochial, sometimes 'her face used to ache with suppressed shrieks' of laughter, it all seemed so remote from real life.

The only man of whom she saw much was her employer. They could talk about Badcock's art acquisitions, the 'Chinese things' that he continued to collect all his life; but in matters of belief they were opposites. He was conventional in all his views, wary of intensity, of 'bad form'. His interest in the arts and in ideas was from outside: he could never be possessed by these things, as she was. However, he was sensitive, aware of people, kind and considerate. She wrote of him in *Pilgrimage* : 'No other dentist was so completely conscious of the patient all the time, as if he were in the chair himself. No other dentist went on year after year remaining sensitive to everything the patient had to endure.'

By comparison, the people with whom she was involved in socialist or nonconformist groups, all wanting to improve the world, were working in terms of abstract values. The personality, the privacy, the sensitivity, the intimations of mortality of individual human beings : these needs were no concern of the reformers. Their approach was more impersonal, she felt, because they were 'the new people ... without upbringing and circumstances ... without backgrounds' ; and 'the worst of these forgotten-truth-restoring heresies is the way they crystallize into fanatical routine in the hands of the disciples'.

Dorothy now believed that there were elements in the present society well worth preserving. The English upper classes at their best, it seemed to her, had created an ethic of honour, compassion and aesthetic and human awareness, compared with which these other movements were essentially cold. Conservatives were 'the best socialists, being liberal-*minded*. Most Socialists were narrow and illiberal, holding on to liberal ideas'. She formulated for herself a position as a 'Tory Anarchist'—someone who wanted to preserve the old virtues, where they truly existed, of decency, duty and tolerance, but also at the same time to see the abuses of social injustice and bureaucracy curbed.

She believed in the supreme importance of the individual ; and she now perceived that the great reforming movements were founded on principles of class or race rather than of individuality. The two forces behind these ideologies were Marx and Tolstoy : the Marxian analysis based upon class, the Tolstoyan on race, on the drive and the movement of peoples, in which the individual is swept along helplessly.

Various religious groups also engaged her for a time, especially the Quakers ; but she never became 'formally a Friend', having been kept out by the sense of her 'inability to engage in social enterprise', though she considered the Friends' ' "organization" the most flexible ever known'.

Unitarianism interested her, but it seemed too cerebral an approach to religion. With its 'cold, humorous intellectuality', it was a rationale of something that must remain essentially non-rational. For a time Catholicism 'seemed seductively to offer a refuge. But it offered also the spectacle of the corrupting influence of power.' Moreover, she found 'the clerics, of all varieties, still for the most part identifying religion with morality'. In later years she summed up her view on this subject: 'So many people identify "religion" with "church". But does not the secret lie with the mystics of all creeds? All the Saints and Mystics bring the same message. Only the whole being of man, rather than any one aspect or quality, whether scientific or artistic or philosophical, is able to investigate the nature of reality.'

Meanwhile, she had also been attracted to the Jewish faith. This was, however, for the sake of a man. There arrived one day at Mrs. Baker's a young man, several years younger than Dorothy, of distinguished appearance, with dark hair and beard, a strange foreign elegance of dress and a courtliness of manner unusual and rather touching in someone so young. This was Benjamin Grad, the son of a successful Jewish lawyer in Russia. He had been ill for a time in Basle, but had come on to London to continue his studies of language and philosophy.

He and Dorothy met and found they had many interests in common. She helped him with his English, and he in turn taught her his method of learning foreign languages. ('He speaks most, and understands all, European languages, and possesses a Bible in each, the sole source, for several of them, of his knowledge, which does not include pronunciation.') His method was to study a page of the Bible in the language he was learning, side by side with the corresponding page in a language he already knew. She proved an apt pupil, with a better ear than his for the languages she learned.

They read philosophy and literature. He introduced her to the work of certain Russian writers whom she had not yet discovered, and they discussed 'the philosophers whom, reading, [she found] more deeply exciting than the novelists'.

24

Learning languages, translating passages, gave her an insight into creative writing, whose mysterious process began to fascinate her; and at times it seemed that 'everything in her life existed only for the sake of the increasing bunch of pencilled half-sheets' of her translations.

Her critical faculties, and her dissatisfaction with most of the novels she read, increased with her interest in writing. And yet a novel could offer an entire individual world of experience, presenting reality, even sometimes history, in terms of human lives. Most novels, however, were mere collections of incidents and sentiments, excluding 'the essential: first-hand life'.

She and Benjamin argued these and other points passionately, as they walked for hours round London. Her knowledge and quickness astounded him. In the Russian–Jewish world that he came from, a world where the Tsarist persecution was reaching its height in the pogroms, learning was exclusively a masculine preserve, and a scholar would often be supported by his wife with a stall or a pushcart in the market. But here was this Englishwoman questioning his intellect, telling him that what he called thinking was merely the collecting of facts and theories; whereas knowledge, for her, was 'bought only by experience. All else is hearsay.'

Her prettiness as well as her intelligence moved him. Another friend wrote of her that 'no one but me can now remember how *pretty* Dorothy was when I first met her— slender and pink and white, and her hair pure gold crushed back in wings each side of her face'. Benjamin began to fall in love with her.

She liked him, his company was pleasant on these walks, with the two of them rushing on faster and faster in the heat of some argument, but sometimes she grew 'tired with thought and speech', with all this talk and these ideas that were well enough as far as they went, but only stopped short of life, and distracted her from what was more important, from seeing things minutely: the streets, people's faces.

His Russian–Jewish character, his warmth and distinctive intellect delighted her, but also made a barrier between them. Just as, in her time at the Hanover school, she had found the life in Germany more vivid than any she had ever known before, and yet it had made her aware of her own essential Englishness and difference, so it was now with Benjamin. She wrote in *Pilgrimage* of this difference, that 'there were things in England with truth shining behind them. English people did not shine. But something shone behind them. Russians shone. But there was nothing behind them.'

With Badcock, who was much less intellectual, there weren't these differences. Her origins had been the same as his, an easy, affluent middle-class background—the background that years before, in Barnes, in the halcyon time before the crash, had been so pleasant that she nearly committed herself to it for life; and now in Badcock's company there was a return to 'those restorative times of ease and orderly living'. She sometimes 'nostalgically searched the new telephone directory for the names' of people she 'used to know in the Barnes district'.

She needed to settle. Her health was weakening, not only because of over-work and malnutrition, but also because of the unnaturalness of her life, the isolation, the frightening moments of wondering what would become of her when she was too old to do her job and live from hand to mouth. At such times 'all seemed darkness within and without'. The past still oppressed her : her mother's illness and her father's disgrace, and before that the years of pretending, of being unlike other people : 'our family, always masquerading.'

One weekend she and Badcock travelled down together to Berkshire, he to his cottage in the Thames valley, she on to Abingdon to stay with relations. The relations were amazed and impressed when the same day he turned up in Abingdon, on a pretext of seeing his relatives there, but clearly to spend the day with Dorothy. They were seeing quite a lot of each other outside surgery hours. It was pleasant to go with him to lectures or concerts. He had all the best English qualities, the decency and tolerance, but none of the depth or intensity of Benjamin.

But Benjamin too, in his different way, was limited. There was something impersonal in his enthusiasms : he had his fixed beliefs. She wrote to his son some years later: 'I believe that intellectual distinction is bought, very generally, at a high cost. My idea of an "intellectual" is a person who as a rule is rather lacking in *intelligence*: i.e. in balance between the rational and emotional faculties.'

Dorothy was finding it hard to 'face up to marriage', and to choose between these men, who both loved her, though neither was altogether suited to her. It seemed to her that women and men at this period of time were too different to have any close understanding. Men were 'practitioners, dealing with things (including "ideas") rather than with people, obliged on every level to *do* rather than to *be*; feebler than women in their sense of being, and knowing almost nothing of women save in relation to themselves'.

She and Benjamin became friendly with the publisher Charles Daniel and his fiancée Florence Woolland. An unconventional publisher, Daniel was often called a crank, but despite some peculiar ideas he was brave and enlightened. His chief author was a woman called Mary Everest Boole, whose writings—on psychology, physiology, mathematics, religion—had a cabbalistic oddness and intensity, and 'who declared, almost, only the mad are sane'. Women's intuition she rated very high in the scale of human faculties. Dorothy was interested and even impressed by her.

Daniel and his fiancée, and Benjamin and Dorothy 'haunted each other incessantly in various weird groups, Tolstoyans, simple-lifers and others'. After Daniel and Florence were married, they kept open house for a wide circle of intellectuals and cranks.

Dorothy, involved with these people, began to draw back from Badcock and his 'enclosures of social life'. It always had jarred on her that he could keep up two separate relationships with her, one personal the other professional, treating her at work with cool detachment. She hated these professional relationships; they seemed to her unnatural, an outrage on humanity. Employer and employee should behave to one another as people. This other approach was what turned human beings into wage slaves, 'tired, helpless bits of the machinery of business life'.

There was no question, any longer, of her marrying Badcock, but still she stayed on as his secretary. As time passed, their relationship settled again into friendship. They continued to care about each other, and to write to each other, to the end of their lives. In later years she took a proprietary interest in his welfare; and once, when he was old, she affectionately took him to task for not writing to tell her that he had grown a beard.

She had a capacity to interest and move people, even on casual acquaintance. Although she was no one in particular and not a great beauty, there was something impressive about her. Badcock's young student brother, sent to inquire at her lodgings one morning when she hadn't turned up at the surgery, found her unwell but setting out for work, and he walked with her to Harley Street. Suddenly out of the blue as they walked along, the boy exclaimed angrily: 'You ought to be supported by the State!' His outburst astonished her. These days she was often unwell, 'her vitality . . . so low' that she had to drag herself through the working day.

Benjamin Grad was now deeply in love with her. She couldn't encourage him: she thought they were different in too many ways. He was generous and patient, however, and their life went on much as before. They were both still at Endsleigh Street, involved to some extent in the life of the house with its constant stream of boarders, among them a series of Canadian doctors, one of whom was interested in her and turned up again in her life some years later.

She and Benjamin still read and translated together, and had their long walks of impassioned discussion, and went on to lectures and meetings as before. He was ardently Zionist, and she too supported this cause. He still hoped that she might return his love. He met some of her friends, and impressed them with his natural dignity, goodness and intelligence. She knew that in his own quiet way he was as wilful as she, and his fixed ideas made him more stubborn. If they were to marry, she would have to be the one to make concessions. She would find herself committed to his way of life, his earnest intellectualism and the patriarchal Jewish family pattern. There could be no half measures in marrying him : she would have to be converted to Judaism, which, like Catholicism, she saw as a 'world of "thou shalt not"'.

However, she was moved by his unworldliness, which put him at the mercy of people. It brought out her strong protective instincts. She wrote of him, as Michael in *Pilgrimage* : 'There are ways in which I like him and am in touch with him as I never could be with an Englishman. Things he understands. And his absolute sweetness. Absence of malice and enmity.' She now believed she loved him, and she gave him her 'provisional pledge'.

But something had been making him uneasy, and he finally admitted to her that in the year he spent in Basle before coming on to England, he had suffered a breakdown and had been in an institution.

The revelation, far from putting her off, made her feel even more protective. She was moved by his distress, and to please him she went to see a woman of whom he had heard, an Englishwoman, formerly a Christian, who had married a Jew and been converted to Judaism. Dorothy, talking to this woman and seeing how sequestered a life she led, realized that she couldn't take on such a rôle. She would have to break out of the enclosure, and the marriage would end in disaster.

Benjamin loved her so much that he would have given way and abandoned his faith, but she couldn't accept such a sacrifice. Still they went on meeting, and walking round London, and arguing and talking as always. Through being in love, she had been herself more freely with him than with anyone before ; and as she wrote later : 'What matters is the illumination coming during this time of being in love. Even when the lovers are mistaken in each other . . . the revelation remains, indestructible.'

Intellectually too he had helped her to broaden her outlook. The translation he had taught her was satisfying work, and at best it was even creative, with the translator working in two different worlds and having to bring the text to life within new frames of reference. She described translating as 'a fascinating job . . . an affair of three processes. First a literal rendering of the whole text to ensure incursiveness. Then, putting the original out of sight, and rewriting in good English, involving frequent finding of equivalents for the untranslatables. Then the whole laid aside for at least a few days (should be *months*) and at last the ultimate rescript.'

From translation, she moved on to writing a story, her first, and she sent it to the magazine *Home Chat*. It was returned 'without thanks'. But a year or two later she wrote a sketch, more personally felt, 'The Russian and his Book'. She sent it to *The Outlook*, and it was accepted and published anonymously in the edition of 4 October 1902.

Always in her life until now, when it came to a choice between one special person and the world outside personal involvement, the impersonal world proved the stronger. It seemed to be going that way once again. London and her life there, her freedom and her untrammelled view of things, meant more to her than Benjamin. It was 'only by the pain of remaining free' that one could 'have the whole world round one all the time'.

She finally broke off the engagement to Benjamin. He left Endsleigh Street, and she was on her own again, feeling a mixture of sadness and relief. She wrote wryly of her unhappiness at this time : 'Always I failed to achieve, try as I would, a complete despair.' Benjamin continued to turn up at intervals in her life, still hoping she might change her mind ; and she was glad not to lose him entirely.

From time to time she visited her family. Her unmarried sister Alice, of whom little is known and who died young in 1910, was still in Wiltshire 'with the sausage Harrises'. The Batchelors now had two children, and Jessie and her husband were still living in Hastings with their small daughter. Dorothy was fond of them all, and her own maternal feelings were engaged by her nephew and nieces ; but she had grown too far away from her family to see very much of them now.

Someone else from her past reappeared at this time. She received a note one morning from her school friend Amy Robbins. Latterly Dorothy had begun to come to terms with the past, which she felt as very present and real, a past 'not recalled but present so that she could move into any part and be there as before'. The past, in this re-living of it, also altered and developed, its people and incidents taking on new meanings. The past, she later wrote, was 'misrepresented in being called "unalterable"'. In re-living it, she found it to be no longer 'a chronological sequence', but composed 'after the manner of a picture, with things in their true proportions and relationships', with many 'completely transformed'.

She had also learned to value the trivia that filled people's lives. As a girl she had always hated small-talk, taking refuge in her 'old sullen silences' whenever there seemed to her nothing worth saying. But it seemed to her now that the ordinary routine and small-talk of people had validity and meaning ; and even their silliness was part of the magical quality of life. But she was more than ever aware that she was outside all this, an onlooker. She had learned to be sociable, but only on the surface. She still couldn't let herself go. Both her shyness ('anything up to ten years it takes me to get to know people') and her critical perceptions prevented her. She still had her old sense of guilt, of something being wrong with her, and something that was hostile to people, her 'old desire to smash their complacency'.

Receiving the note from Amy Robbins took her back to her schooldays, when she had been one of the brightest girls and head of the school, and yet insecure, so that she greatly admired Amy's sureness, her 'bolder curiosity' and scientific cleverness. Amy too had had a family disaster. Her father had been killed in a railway accident shortly after she left Southborough House. But Amy—now to be called 'Jane', it seemed—had never flagged in her course. She continued her studies, working towards the London B.Sc. degree ; and then she had married, and she seemed very pleased with her life, although there was a hint of some trouble.

The two school friends met in a tea shop in London, and Dorothy found her as pretty as ever—in her husband's description, a 'fragile figure, with very delicate features, very fair hair and very brown eyes'—and as sure of her beliefs.

31

Dorothy, by contrast, still felt as uncertain and awkward as when they were girls. But Jane admired her courage and the free life she led as an emancipated woman on her own.

Jane also had behaved independently. Her husband had been married when she met him as one of his students at a London tutorial college. For a time she had lived with him, until his first wife had divorced him. Jane, believing in his talent as a writer, had defied the conventions of Barnes, and won over her mother, who at one point had mortgaged her house to buy furniture for the young couple.

Jane's husband had been the son of a woman in service, and then worked behind a counter in a shop. He was largely self-educated. He had married his cousin, an attractive and sweet-natured girl who understood none of his ambitions. Through Jane, he had broken away from his old life and started to concentrate on writing, first essays and stories, and then in 1895—the year of his marriage to Jane— he had published his first two novels. His name was Herbert George Wells.

Wells and Jane had recently moved to Worcester Park in Surrey, where Dorothy was now invited to visit them. The prospect of meeting new people always made her uneasy. But Wells was very friendly; a short, stocky, sandy-haired man with a bright, assured, positive manner. Everything he said, in his high squeaky voice with its traces of Cockney, was amusing and clever. His face was rather plain; but in spite of his commonplace appearance, he had remarkable presence.

Physically Dorothy found him a little repellent, and yet there was something about him that drew her attention : she couldn't stop watching him and listening, fascinated, to his brilliant patter and pronouncements—even though she disagreed with almost all he said.

He talked of history and science. The two, to him, were virtually one. The gods were the heritage of primitive man's fear of natural phenomena, and offered only 'vague promises of helpful miracles for the cheating of simple souls'. The romantic myths—all this 'he and she' stuff in novels and plays—were likewise meaningless. Women and men had a biological function to fulfil for each other, and ways of giving pleasure to each other, both sexually and as companions, within the biological pattern.

Like Dorothy he had attended Fabian meetings, and he was beginning to formulate his own opposition to the party line as preached by Shaw, and more particularly by Webb with his theoretical, bureaucratic socialism. Wells, always dynamic in his beliefs, felt that socialism should achieve political power in England, and that more young people should be recruited to its cause. Scientific socialism was his creed; he had now put aside the earlier, more questioning view that he had expressed in his first published essay, 'The Rediscovery of the Unique' (1891), asserting the uniqueness of all Being and the existence of something ineffable beyond science.

He loved an audience, and he was very gregarious. At week-ends the house was full of people, many of them writers, teachers or social reformers. Jane, a skilful hostess, presided over all their bright talk. Dorothy, suddenly bored and depressed by it all, forgot her shyness, and launched an attack on some idea that Wells had just been elucidating. To his 'fury', she 'dared to oppose to his scientific socialism' the thesis of a book she had just read, Benjamin Kidd's *Social Evolution* (1894). Kidd believed that religion, not science, was the cornerstone of history, and that even political and social reforms should stem from religious beliefs.

It was the first of many arguments between Wells and Dorothy. She told him subsequently that his dogma was as rigid as any theologian's, and equally incomplete, since Wells 'saw all he approved in terms of its qualities and all else in terms of its defects'. He was a 'dazzled disciple of Huxley', and couldn't 'accept the tragedy of freedom'. He was 'essentially fascist', and 'the Ants' were 'his ideal community, fascism perfectly realized'. He wanted to regiment mankind into a 'pathetically naive and unimaginative' Utopia.

According to Wells, this Utopia was to be an oligarchy ruled by ideal people whom he called 'Samurai'. Membership of this class would be 'regulated by the filtering processes of education and of the tests of social life', and baser strains would be rigorously excluded. In the thirties, re-affirming this early thesis, he was to write that 'the appearance of such successful organizations as the Communist Party and the Italian Fascists' had greatly strengthened his 'belief in the essential soundness of this conception of the governing order of the future'.

His ideals also included free love. He had rebelled against Victorian morality, in which the 'helplessly young' were not only being 'jammed for life into laborious, tedious, uninteresting and hopeless employments, but they were being denied the most healthy and delightful freedoms of mutual entertainment'.

His ideas, so torrential and brilliant, were in practice sometimes contradictory and muddled. He had always had an ideal dream of goddess-like women, a 'fantasy of free, ambitious, self-reliant women who would mate with me and go their way, as I desired to go my way'. In practice, his worship of women and his sexual desires were separate. Jane he admired and loved, and, in his own words, they 'worked in close association and sympathy' but with 'no such sexual fixation' as, ironically, he still had for his first wife. So Jane had to play the game his way, be complaisant, charm his friends and his mistresses. He was devoted to her, but he wasn't monogamous. For all his rebellion against the old morality, most women were to him, essentially, what they had been to most Victorian men : 'an object of pleasure, incidentally a biological contrivance, and/or a household necessity', but essentially subservient, with their individuality needing to be kept in its place. He was successful with women. He had many affairs, and some of his women, when he had lost interest in them sexually, would be turned into handmaidens—canvassers or helpers at meetings or with clerical work.

In these early years of his marriage to Jane, he often felt hemmed in by domesticity. He would go off alone on long bicycle rides round the countryside. In Dorothy, whose brilliance annoyed and intrigued him, and who also attracted him physically, he began to think he saw his ideal. But to her, his belief that the species mattered more than the individual, and his view of humanity as 'merely a stage in an automatic "evolution" ', showed him to be her old familiar enemy, whom she must oppose.

In 1898 he had a recurrence of his earlier consumptive illness. These attacks, together with the turmoil of his personal life and his half-fulfilled ambitions, his feeling that perhaps he would never be a widely popular writer, caused him to break down completely. Devotedly Jane nursed him back to health in the seaside town of Sandgate; and here, in 1900, with his fortunes improving, he had a new house built for them, with a garden to the sea.

Dorothy was still a frequent visitor, and still she and Wells disputed endlessly; but she was fond of him. It was probably she who with Jane played Beethoven piano duets to him by the hour when he felt depressed. In turn, he and Jane 'were kind, alive to one's life in a way other people were not'.

So his strange, prolonged courtship of Dorothy continued. Her feminism, which was not too vehement, also appealed to him and moved him. In these still early days of the Suffragette campaign, he could write of 'this growing demand on the part of women for economic and political independence', that 'it seemed to me that here at last advancing upon me was that great-hearted free companionship of noble women of which I had dreamed from my earliest years'.

This companionship he was finding with Dorothy, in spite of their disputes. Physically he had become more attractive. Improved health had given him a better colour, and his features had a smoother, less unfinished look. His manner had always been engaging; and now that his books had begun to be successful, he was more than ever the enthusiast, given to voluble monologues and gestures.

Dorothy had no intention of having an affair with him. Apart from her feelings of loyalty to Jane, she thought him incapable of caring very deeply for people. 'Persons could not exist for him', since 'he made no distinction between "individual", a biological category, and "person", a spiritual category.'

However, he pursued her with a mixture of cunning and naiveté. He was very disarming, and began to show more of an interest in the details of her life, her work, the shifting population at Endsleigh Street, the women's club, the Arachne, that she had lately joined so as to be able to entertain her sisters and friends, like her former pupil from Finsbury Park, when they came up to London.

She took refuge from Wells in her London activities, her reading and translating, and her friendships with people like Winifred Ray, a girl who believed in her talent and urged her to attempt a novel. Instead, for a lark she and Winifred compiled a 'nonsense news-sheet, the House-holder's Handy Compendium', with ridiculous 'Hints' and 'Classified' columns.

Her visits to the Wells's were less frequent, but both of them wrote to her regularly. She and Wells, since the beginning of their friendship, had been in the habit of writing argumentative notes to each other—hers attacking his books and his ideas—and now his letters began to be tender. Dorothy found that she missed him, with his wit and his charm, his kindness and good humour in the face of her attacks on his cherished ideas. He was more important in her life than she had thought he could be.

To her dismay, he carried his pursuit of her into her own London territory. She was afraid that his worldly viewpoint would destroy all the spell of it. He would see only the muddle and the shabbiness of her life and the people she was close to in London.

In 1903 he had joined the Fabian Society; and in February 1906 he launched his attack on the old guard of the Society with his paper 'The Faults of the Fabians'. He then went on a lecture tour to America, returning determined to try to reorganize the Society, to get more political meaning and more life into it, rally the younger socialists to more positive action, and sweep away the bureaucratic approach of the Webbs and Shaw.

He returned also to the start of his affair with Dorothy.

She had given in, at last. The first time he made love to her left her an impression that 'he was rather ugly without his clothes'. None the less, they suited each other. This 'love-affair, growing increasingly beyond the limits of the *passade* which had been agreed upon between him and Jane' was 'especially embarrassing and dangerous because it could not be kept secret in this small gossiping Society'. It was Wells's invariable habit to destroy private letters; but hers he now started to keep. He also introduced her to his father, living in retirement in Hampshire, and she liked the old man's 'gruff sturdy forthrightness and independence'.

Her character was softening from its old inviolability. She was growing more feminine, and she began to think of having a place of her own, instead of the invariable lodging-house room. A chance offered itself through a new acquaintance, Miss Moffatt, whom she met at the Arachne Club.

Miss Moffatt, an impoverished gentlewoman of about forty, large and imperious and 'always *angry* in her outlooks', but with a genteel admiration for the arts and a somewhat heavy girlish charm, was an L.C.C. teacher of evening classes. 'Deceived by Dorothy's modest appearance', seeing her as 'artistic' and well-read, she suggested that they might share a flat.

Dorothy liked the idea. It would be an economy, if they could find something cheap. She would be able to save a little more to help her family. Miss Moffatt, who was clever with her needle and made all the blouses that invariably clothed her bulky form, could make their curtains : another economy. She was an indomitable woman, in her way, as 'she set her teeth at everything and battled on', and she liked to say, half-way through a task : 'I've broken the back of *that*.'

Dorothy liked her well enough, but they were different sorts of people, and that would be a safeguard against an over-intimate friendship. Miss Moffatt's well-bred manner, her upper-class reserve and discretion, would also help to preserve a certain detachment between them.

They found a flat, newly converted, in a St. Pancras slum street. It was so damp that 'beards grew' on their luggage.

D

When they quickly gave notice, the landlord burst into tears, begging them to stay. His daughter was an art student, he explained, and he needed the money to support her through her course. But his tenants managed to resist these persuasions, and left after a fortnight.

A few streets away from Endsleigh Gardens was an alleyway, a slum, connecting Upper Woburn Place with a network of mean, noisy streets round a patch of waste ground. The alleyway, Woburn Buildings (now Woburn Way), backed on to the waste ground and consisted of two opposite terraces of small, narrow eighteenth-century houses facing each other across a flagged pavement with no right of way for vehicles. The houses were dilapidated but pretty, with bow-fronted shop-windows and wrought-iron balconies at the first-floor level. Above the second storeys were box-like attics. At 2 Woburn Buildings, over the shop of 'Francis Cook, sculpture cleaner', the two women found cheap rooms : the two second-floor ones front and back, and the attic.

The rooms were cramped, but they had character, 'retaining, in their decrepitude, something of an ancient dignity and, with the faded painted ceilings of their main rooms, a touch of a former splendour'. As they worked to get the rooms in order, the two women weren't too depressed by the squalor of the neighbourhood, the stench of tom-cat and rubbish that rose up from the small enclosed partitions of garden and the waste ground at the back, and the noises late at night of revellers straggling home drunk from the nearby public houses.

What was harder for Dorothy to bear was the smug narrowness of outlook that began to show in her flatmate. In the cramped quarters of these rooms, in the heat of this 'torrid summer', the petty irritations and slights became magnified ; but Dorothy tried very hard to be tolerant. Yet she was always entirely honest. Miss Moffatt was bound to find out about Dorothy's affair 'with a married man', and she was predictably shocked and disgusted. Dorothy now seemed to her 'everything undesirable'.

Relations between the two women were strained, but they

managed to weather these ups and downs. Some months had passed, and they were still in the flat. For Dorothy it was a compensation that she was near to all her Bloomsbury haunts, no more than a few minutes' walk from the first of the squares. But the view from their attic, above the slum rooftops, took in the grim towers of St. Pancras.

In 18 Woburn Buildings, directly across the alleyway, a man of about forty, a 'tall pervading figure', pale and dark-haired, could often be seen writing by the light of 'two immensely tall, thick white candles, giving the dimly visible background the air of a deserted shrine'. It was W. B. Yeats. Dorothy noticed him sometimes in the street, or in the distance crossing one of the squares, and his face seemed familiar.

Walking home one night through a nearby square, in the darkness she didn't at first see him coming towards her down the path, the 'tall cloaked figure with dark hair ebullient above a pallid brow'; and he too was preoccupied, so that they nearly collided. Standing aside, he stared into her face, with 'something approaching a glimmer of recognition', in his eyes an expression 'of a man aged and astray in sorrow'. She nearly spoke to him, but instead she nodded and passed on in silence. Through that summer and autumn they continued to see each other across the narrow alley separating their windows, but neither ever broke the silence. 'For memory,' she wrote, 'we stand permanently confronted either side of that lake of moonlight in the square.'

Now, with the days drawing in, in the autumn of 1906, and the bleakness of the place becoming more and more depressing, she thought longingly of her old room at Mrs. Baker's, and the sense of anonymity and freedom in that house.

Charles Daniel had started a new periodical—*Crank: an Unconventional Magazine*, he called it—and he asked Dorothy to write book reviews regularly for it, the first of which appeared in the number of August 1906. She found it daunting at first, to have to pass judgment in print on someone else's work, into which years of toil and thought might have gone. She spent hours doing background

39

reading, before she felt qualified to write her reviews. Even then, as she later wrote, she 'went nearly mad with responsibility and the awfulness of discovering the way words express almost nothing at all'. In time she gained more facility, but she was still immensely conscientious in reviewing.

She wrote her reviews in clear, unpretentious language, and her judgments were firm but sympathetic. As journalistic pieces these reviews were far from brilliant, since she was too concerned to do justice to the work to expand her own writing personality. This question of the writer's personality, how much or how little it ought to obtrude, had always occupied her; and the over-obtrusiveness of novelists had spoiled many works for her. 'Always . . . one was aware of the author and applauding, or deploring, his manipulations.'

Meanwhile her affair with Wells was causing increasing scandal in the Fabian Society. Wells, blundering on with his mixture of courage and insensitivity, both in the affair itself and in his battle with the leading Fabians, took little account of the tide of public opinion against him. There were stormy Fabian meetings at Clifford's Inn, with shouted interruptions and bursts of applause—an excitement that infected the whole movement for a time. Wells was questioning the premature rush to democracy, which in his view was a principle that Socialism had taken from Marxism, with its positing of the Class War as inevitable and basic to progress. Glibly, and blindly, in his view, the Webbs were urging the early Trade Union officials to enter Parliament and become leaders of the State, 'though if you only looked at and listened to a few of them—!'

His love affair with Dorothy inevitably reflected these conflicts and uncertainties. She wanted to end the affair, but it wasn't the moment to let him down. His Fabian struggle was coming to a crisis, and he knew he was handling it badly. Shaw was a far more effective public speaker, whereas Wells would get tangled in his own over-abundant ideas, and would bluster and babble. Dorothy saw that with 'the peculiar qualities that do him such disservice on a platform and are in a room so immutably effective', he was losing his battle.

In her own life, the experiment of sharing a flat had proved a failure; another dead end. She questioned the change of direction in her life in these past years. Before then, she had managed, through years of privation, to keep her separate vision intact in a 'solitude . . . very different from loneliness'. Now it was threatened by this easier world of social pleasures, her club, her own flat and a love affair. What had been the point of all that solitude and hardship, if now she was giving up those depths for a life lived more shallowly? She had always felt instinctively—an attitude inherited, perhaps, from her Richardson forebears—that the hard path, the deeper side of life with its loneliness and losses and 'tragedy', in the end offered most. She wanted to have 'a life not astray in ceaseless movement'. Related to her view that personal relationships were sometimes a distraction from life, was an idiosyncratic belief of hers that people should sit side by side and not facing each other. They could be more relaxed if they were free to see everything going on round them, and not have the view blocked by one another's faces.

At the Arachne Club one day in August 1906, at about the time that her first review was published in Daniel's 'vivid, if obscure anarchist monthly', Dorothy became aware that a girl, a new resident whom she had not seen before, was observing her intently. Presently the girl came and spoke to her, talking about herself very spontaneously. She had been studying art in Paris, and now in London she was training to be an actress—at the Royal Academy of Dramatic Art, she said. She was only a month past her twenty-first birthday and remarkably pretty, with fine, firmly-cut features. Her character emerged as a mixture of naiveté, absurdity and sophistication, as she poured out her story of family opposition, love affairs, ideals. She had had the courage to break away from a protective family background in Worcestershire. Her father was a surgeon, well-off and with County aspirations, not unlike Charles Richardson. He had been led to spend too much on all the paraphernalia of riding, hunting and shooting, and to keep up an establishment somewhat beyond his means, but not disastrously so.

There were four sons and two daughters. Veronica—Avice-Veronica Leslie-Jones—had been the pet of the family. This was fortunate, since her artistic ambitions didn't greatly please her father. But one of her elder brothers—who had been successful in India and used to come home on leave like a nabob, 'a latter-day Jos Sedley'—had made her an allowance, enabling her to study in Paris and now to subsist in digs in London, at the Arachne Club.

Before settling in London, she had gone with her family on a holiday to Symonds Yat in Herefordshire, and there she had fallen tremendously in love. She did nothing by halves: her emotions, enthusiasms, friendships, dislikes were all excessive, so that all her life she moved 'from drama to drama'. But the man, who was in the Department of Woods and Forests, was not free to marry her. The romance had had to end, leaving her wretched for a time.

Having told her all this, the girl seemed to feel it gave her a claim on Dorothy. So began a friendship as intense as all Veronica's relationships had to be. Her directness and impulsiveness, the speed with which she established an intimacy, were somewhat disconcerting—but touching and exciting as well. She was very much the actress in her dealings with people, but she had an essentially generous nature.

Her feelings for Dorothy, which included a kind of hero-worship, were possessive: she wanted no one else to be as close to her as she was. Meanwhile, she had also embarked on another ill-fated love affair. This man, Philip, who was many years older than herself, died in the following year. But her friendship with Dorothy engaged her more intensely than her love affair with Philip.

Wherever she went, she talked freely about her own affairs, disarming even the upright Miss Moffatt, who thought she was sweet, and a helpless victim of a much older man, and exclaimed: 'How your parents come to *allow* you to go in for the theatrical profession!' Confidentially Miss Moffatt urged her to emigrate, to get away from Dorothy's influence and find a husband 'who would never know'. This advice amused and delighted Veronica, as any attention to herself always did.

Veronica had been drawn to the Suffragettes, devoting herself to their cause with her usual intensity, dramatic flair and ardour. The fight for woman's suffrage was at a critical stage. She took part in a number of public demonstrations and marches, became a friend of the Pankhursts and 'at one moment of her wild career sang hymns' of protest 'in the streets of Manchester'. Through her, Dorothy, though no militant, took a closer interest in the cause, so that for a time, as she wrote, it 'diverted me from all else'.

In 1903 Jessie and Jack Hale with their small daughter Nathalie had emigrated, settling in Texas. Their departure was a blow to Dorothy, and added to her sense of isolation. Her friendship with Veronica, who was as close to her now as Jessie once had been, filled the gap. At first she had felt a protective indulgence for her, as for a charming wayward child : 'Babinka', she called her. But now there was a bond of intuitive sympathy between them, and they often thought alike and had the same responses to people.

Dorothy now tried to end the Wells affair—only to find that she was pregnant. She wasn't altogether sorry ; she had strong maternal feelings, as she had found with her nieces and nephew. Describing her feelings when she tended a friend's baby, she wrote : 'You have the world in your arms.' A child of her own was a fulfilment she longed for. Wells, delighted by the news of her pregnancy, intended to help her financially. But she wanted only to be finished with him now. She would manage on her own.

Ill at the outset of her pregnancy, her health already poor after years of malnutrition, she still had to struggle through the long days at Harley Street. She wanted to be done with that too. She had worked there for over ten years, and she and Badcock were still friends, but it was a waste of her life,

43

this 'routine work that could not engage the essential forces' of her being. She wanted to devote herself more to her writing, instead of always being so tired and unwell. Time was passing; she was now in her thirties.

At home at Woburn Buildings, the atmosphere was wearing her down; and the presence of Veronica seemed to have made matters worse with Miss Moffatt. In the sickness of pregnancy, she found the place unbearable, the alleyway more stifling, the rooms more cramped than ever. Her whole situation was a trap—Wells, her job, and the sharing of this flat with a woman whose moods alternated between over-friendliness and coldness. She must somehow find the strength to break free.

As Easter of 1907 approached, Dorothy began to have 'pains', as if her labour were going to begin. Veronica, carrying a banner in the Suffragette march of Easter Sunday, was among those arrested and taken to Holloway Prison, where Dorothy visited her. In the grim prison, its conditions unrelieved as yet by liberal reforms, the suffragettes were callously treated and herded among hardened criminals, some of them diseased. When the suffragettes fasted, they were forcibly fed—a process as humiliating as it was painful.

It was after this visit to Holloway Prison that Dorothy's child miscarried. The details she always kept secret, but this was the end of her love affair with Wells. He also resigned from the Fabian Society in the following year. By then he and Jane, and Dorothy, had gone back to being friends again, a friendship that continued for the rest of their lives. He had many subsequent affairs, which Jane always accepted; though a dozen years later she took rooms of her own in Bloomsbury, 'rooms I never saw', Wells wrote in his autobiography. 'She explained what she wanted and I fell in with her idea; and in this secret flat, quite away from all the life that centred upon me, she thought and dreamt and wrote and sought continually and fruitlessly for something she felt she had lost of herself or missed or never attained'.

In the spring of 1907, when Veronica came out of

prison, Dorothy left Woburn Buildings at last, and moved back to 7 Endsleigh Street, where Veronica had previously taken a room. She was worn and dispirited, but glad to be back at Mrs. Baker's. Later, in *Pilgrimage* she wrote of the joy of returning to this house, which she loved. She was in her old attic room, and Veronica had a larger room overlooking the garden at the back of the house.

They spent several months together at Endsleigh Street. For Dorothy this close proximity began to be a strain, despite her great affection for her friend. Veronica was an exhausting companion with her moods and intensity, which were so extreme that her son would find 'too vivid' the account that Dorothy later wrote of Veronica as she was at this time. Dorothy was discovering that she 'shared . . . the masculine dislike and suspicion of women'. Pettiness especially was a fault of women more than men, because of women's closeness to detail, to the 'small but important realities of life'.

But Veronica also was intelligent, and interested in politics and social questions other than women's rights. She had joined the Labour Party very shortly after it evolved out of the Fabian Society in 1903. At this point, her family, disapproving of her ideas and way of life, prevailed upon her brother to cut off her allowance. They wanted her at home, to do the flowers, ride to hounds and make a marriage in the County. Determined not to yield, she worked instead as a skivvy at Endsleigh Street, doing household chores for Mrs. Baker, in return for her keep. For a spoilt girl, who had never lacked money to live on, it was a brave stand ; and hardship improved her. She began to shed some of her affectations.

But Dorothy felt constricted by this close and demanding affection, this 'unrequited love', as Veronica herself later described it. It was another trap from which Dorothy had to break free, as she had done on previous occasions, though each time the struggle left her more tired and damaged. Her health was still poor, and she was troubled by a sense of time passing and nothing accomplished.

Her writing had not yet amounted to much. Apart from

her reviews, and that sketch of 'The Russian and his Book', she had written some articles on socialism and anarchism for Daniel's periodical—'serving her apprenticeship', as she called it—but nothing creative. Her career had no obvious direction, and her personal life even less. She could sum it up as 'London, clerical work, "freedom". The Quest. Love, all sorts, art, all sorts, religion, all sorts.'

Of all the people who had been close to her, Benjamin had most nearly drawn her out of her solitude. She saw him occasionally. His personal life was unsettled; and his intellect, like hers, was always searching for a suitable outlet. Increasingly he found it in Zionism. But in his dealings with people he still needed protection: he had kept his extraordinary innocence of life.

Dorothy wondered whether he and Veronica, who were so different from each other, might find an attraction in those differences. What they had in common was a single-minded toughness that made them survivors. So she introduced them, and they were attracted to each other, initially because of the connexion with Dorothy.

Soon after this meeting, Veronica's lover died suddenly. On learning of his death, she wept uncontrollably all through the night; and Dorothy shared her bed, trying to quieten her. Towards morning Dorothy suddenly said to her: '*Now* you can marry Benjamin.'

Veronica and Benjamin began to see more of each other. He asked her to marry him, and she consented. But it was Dorothy whom they both loved, by Veronica's own account. There was now the question of his breakdown in Switzerland, the memory of which had so troubled him during his engagement to Dorothy. Now it was longer ago, and he did not tell Veronica about it; and Dorothy, debating with herself, felt it wasn't for her to interfere.

She herself was very near a breakdown. She took leave of absence from her job, and at last 'in 1907 . . . escaped into the country', going down to Sussex to stay as a paying guest on a farm on Windmill Hill near Herstmonceux.

The house, called Mount Pleasant, was low-built and rambling, and its setting was beautiful. From this high downland there was a view across woods and fields and marshes to the sea, 'a blue line on a seven-mile-off horizon'.

Miss Penrose ran the house for her family. Her two brothers farmed Scripp and Cowbeech farms, nearby. They were Quakers. There was a Friends' Meeting House in Gardner Street in the pleasant village of Herstmonceux, and through the Penroses, Dorothy was again drawn to Quakerism. She travelled up to town to attend the Friends' 'great annual gathering, the London yearly meeting . . . as an outsider', sitting, on this 'sweltering midsummer evening, in a sloping gallery almost under the roof'; and she found it a moving experience. A few years later, in 1914, she published an anthology of *Gleanings from the Works of George Fox* and a treatise on *The Quakers Past and Present*, describing this work in her Foreword as 'primarily an attempt at showing the position of the Quakers in . . . the family of the mystics'.

Settled in this pleasant Quaker household in Sussex, and living in the country for the first time since her childhood, she was very much attracted to the family and their life. From being a boarder with the Penroses, she soon became one of the family, helping with various chores in the orchard or greenhouse, sharing their closeness to the seasons and the weather, 'the perfect cycle of the year, the good farm year'.

The elder of the brothers, who bore 'the scars of an ill-fated romance', paid court to her, taking her along to sit 'at his side on the box seat of a most decrepit wagonette' on his marketing trips selling his fruit, vegetables and flowers in the coastal towns of Eastbourne, Brighton, Hastings and St. Leonards. He also took her to an auction sale held in the country nearby, a great day in the lives of the simple rustic people who came from miles round. An old farmer's stock and equipment were for sale; and Penrose was intent on acquiring some machinery that he could not otherwise have afforded. It was a simple occasion, but to Dorothy a perfect, unforgettable day.

She interrupted her stay in October to go up to London for the wedding of Veronica and Benjamin. She, who had brought them together, must now give them up to each other. They had taken a villa in Sedgemere Avenue in the North London suburb of Finchley, and Veronica set herself to learn the rôle of housewife. Writing years later she affirmed that she had married Benjamin for Dorothy's sake, and 'Benjamin knew why I married him . . . Benjamin loved Dorothy, but he wanted to marry anyway and above all he wanted a son . . . I never pretended to be in love with my husband.'

Dorothy was ready again to move on. The time in Sussex had helped her to a partial recovery; but it was too small a corner to hold her, and these people were too limited in outlook. As for her association with the Friends, she was still an outsider, for 'the artist's link with religion is nearly quite entirely aesthetic . . . and . . . therefore "they" won't have us inside'. She had to continue her search for her own individual place. The money she had left from her savings was enough for her to travel to Switzerland in January 1908.

Adelboden was a pleasant resort, much frequented by well-to-do English. The complete change of scene, the air, the clarity of light, in this 'enchanted fortnight', made her feel intensely well. With amusement she observed all the strata of people : the English and foreigners, the sporting types, those who were not quite accepted. But there was a camaraderie about most of those on holiday here ; and they welcomed her into their round of sport and outings and pleasant social life.

With this new surge of energy, she wrote a descriptive sketch of that Sussex auction. It was a slight but vivid piece, the most creative work that she had yet done. She sent it to Arthur Baumann, editor of the London *Saturday Review*. It was accepted, and appeared anonymously in the issue of 13 June 1908. It was the first of some thirty such pieces that she wrote in the next five years, for *The Saturday Review*.

Many of these sketches or 'middles' were on Sussex themes ; and on returning to England from Switzerland, she went back to stay at the farm on Windmill Hill. Having got back her health and her strength, she had resolved that her life would be different and that she would achieve something. She had finished with Harley Street, though she still kept in touch with Badcock, and she subsequently used the knowledge she had acquired to write articles and reviews for the *Dental Record*. It was now her aim to make her living by writing.

She struggled on like this—('fantastic venturings, when, in order to go on writing I lived for years on end on less than £1 per week')—in Sussex and then again in London. She was poorer than in her first Bloomsbury days, but she was free, and she was doing what she wished—though not doing it well enough as yet.

Baumann encouraged her to write a novel. His co-editor, Harold Hodge, was more discouraging, as was Wells. She wasn't very certain herself that she could do it, or wanted to. Most novels seemed to have too much dead matter, too much that seemed 'added, intruding, bulging'.

However, she planned several novels, 'each founded on an "Idea". Somehow too easy . . . distasteful and boring.' She would write part of the novel, and then feel bored and dissatisfied with what she was doing, with her 'mass of material . . . expanding in the mind unmanageably, choked by the necessities of narrative'. It was all too facile, too much formula writing—this deliberate planning and setting out of narrative, incidents, characters. None of what she wrote seemed alive; and the 'idea' or theme was useless as a starting point. Ideas were subjective things, variable according to a writer's particular views; and she wanted to 'express the immutable'.

But how—in a novel? She believed that the artist should be 'next door to the mystic as an investigator, because the veil over reality is, for him, almost transparent'. Bunyan, and the mystics, could express the eternal. They wrote what they knew, out of absolute experience, directly, without all this planning and plotting of the work. But theirs were not novels; and she was now struggling to find a way of conveying such reality and immediacy in a novel.

She worked on, without succeeding in her aim, into 1911. The material—scenes and people entirely real—would form itself in her mind, but she couldn't get it through the stifling barrier of narrative conventions. Narrative was 'too technical, dependent on a whole questionable set of agreements and assumptions between reader and writer'.

She thought that Henry James, in *The Ambassadors*, had come very near to breaking through the barrier to a more direct communication. But later, she would write of James : 'His style, fascinating at a first meeting for me, can only be very vulgarly described as a non-stop waggling of the backside as he hands out, on a salver, sentence after sentence, that yet, if the words had no meaning, would weave its own spell. So what? one feels, reaching the end of the drama in a resounding box, where no star shines and no bird sings.'

Nor did she care greatly for the 'work of art' type of novel. She preferred Trollope and Jane Austen for 'their complete non-literariness', and gave her fullest praise to Dostoievsky 'who is human history and prophecy in one'.

Working at her novel, she managed to eke out a living by doing more articles, translations and proof reading. On returning to London from Sussex, she had wanted to make a fresh start, and so had moved out of Bloomsbury, taking a room in a Y.W.C.A. hostel in St. John's Wood, then still an almost rustic part of London with its tree-lined streets of large old villas set in spacious gardens.

This hostel was just such a villa; and its character as well as its setting appealed to her. It was inhabited by many nationalities, as Endsleigh Street had been; and she soon felt at home and made friends with the other women here. She was easier with people nowadays, and her magnetism had not diminished. ('There were so many young girls who fell for Dorothy', Veronica wrote of this time, adding : 'I don't mean that in any "not nice" way.') The other girls, gravitating round Dorothy, vied for her notice.

She looked younger than her age; not as slender as before, but her hair was still golden and thick, and her complexion still fresh. She had the cachet of being a writer; and in talking she used words with wit and precision, so that people liked to listen to her—the more so because of her beautiful voice, the 'Bernhardt voice', another friend called it, and her throwaway, ironic humour.

A Russian girl, Olga Sokoloff, was fascinated by her. This friend of Kropotkin, who was then living in St. John's Wood 'and with whom she had "much talkings" ', was a girl of affluent background who had become an ardent revolutionary. She was studying in England, and finding the English unapproachable and inexpressive. She fastened on Dorothy as someone totally different from this type.

But Olga, intense and unhappy, suddenly went off to Paris with a lover. Disappointed in the affair, one evening in Paris she scribbled a postcard of farewell to Dorothy. '*Perhaps* there are better dreams,' she wrote on the card, quoting Wells's *Sea Lady*—and then she killed herself.

Death was in the air. The First World War was casting its shadow before it. The old conventional patterns of society were breaking apart. Spreading from the so-called bohemian world, there was a strange new hectic atmosphere in London's social life. Behaviour was freer and pleasures had a desperate gaiety about them.

In 1912 Dorothy became friendly with the novelist J. D. Beresford and his wife Beatrice. Jack Beresford had published several novels, most of them committed to some theme or idea. He urged Dorothy to try again to write a novel.

The Beresfords had a house in St. Ives, and nearby a cottage converted from an old ruined chapel. They pressed Dorothy to come down and stay with them. Living was cheaper in Cornwall than in London. If she wished, she could live in the chapel, and write undisturbed. The chapel was said to be haunted, but she wouldn't mind that.

Dorothy was now forty. She still hadn't found a way of writing that satisfied her, and this was perhaps a last chance that she couldn't let pass. She liked St. Ives, from her visits to the Beresfords, who were so hospitable that staying with them gave her a sense of 'blissful irresponsibility'. So she went, and met Beresford's friend Hugh Walpole, also staying there. When the three of them walked, talking eagerly, up on to the cliffs overlooking the rough coast, it made her remember her childhood holidays in Dawlish and Weymouth. This West Country coast had a satisfying ruggedness. She felt that she might work well here, in this atmosphere.

Friends thought that Walpole had asked her to marry him; but if he did, she declined. She was now single-minded about writing. She moved into the old, haunted chapel; and the first time she was alone in the house, with the back door locked, she thought she heard the ghost. But when she went down to the kitchen, there was nobody there. She was 'enchanted' with her ghost. Otherwise, she was entirely alone. No one ever called, except once a week a woman with a few bare necessities of food and supplies. Dorothy existed on scraps, with an occasional jar of tongue from which she would cut herself a slice when she was hungry and when she had a moment to spare from her writing. 'Suddenly the world had dropped away. But never had humanity been so close. Everything took on a terrific intensity.' Never before had she been so free of distractions; and she wrote fast and fluently.

But it was only to realize yet again, on re-reading her pages, that they had no life. They were just like other novels, the ones that always left her unsatisfied, feeling that there was no reality in them, because they were 'written for the reader, things explained showmanwise'.

She had wanted her novel to be a living entity in its own right apart from its author, instead of merely having a reported, reflected reality. The novelist's presence ought to be a translucent one, not something blocking the view of the world he created in his novel. A novel should be written as a life should be lived, with a clear and unflagging awareness. She hadn't begun to achieve such a light of reality in what she had written so far.

She threw away the batch of dead pages. Nothing really happened in them, no one existed apart from the author stringing together words and incidents to very little effect. If only she could learn to express real experience, as if at first hand, it would be far more exciting and vivid than any made-up plot.

She was searching for an entirely new method: 'The material that moved me to write would not fit the framework of any novel I had experienced. I believed myself to be, even when most enchanted, intolerant of the romantic and the realist novel alike. Each, so it seemed to me, left out certain essentials and dramatized life misleadingly.'

Perhaps she might use her own life as the basis of her novel—not reporting exactly what had happened, but transmuting experience and characters through a new viewpoint, not the novelist's. She would have to select, and make adjustments and changes, to fit the new consciousness that would be the centre of her novel. She must create that new persona, a narrator very like herself and yet independent of her. She, the author, must abdicate from her own position at the centre of the story she was telling, and leave the field to Miriam, her narrator.

With the first words, Miriam must be on her own, pushed out into the tide of her life, and the reader there with her ; and the whole of what followed—events and perceptions—must be refracted through Miriam and told in her voice alone. ('I suddenly realized that I couldn't go on in the usual way, talking *about* Miriam, describing her. There she was as I first saw her, going upstairs. But who was *there* to *describe* her? It came to me suddenly. It was an extraordinary moment when I realized what could and what could not be done. Then it became more and more thrilling as I saw what *was* there.')

The reader must also be made to surrender his identity and live for a while completely through Miriam's being. The incompleteness with which this had previously been done was, for her, the failure of most novels. A novel should illuminate consciousness, and wake people up to their own individual world, that too often stayed darkened and unknown through the whole of a lifetime. The novelist, by setting out one human world in depth, should show them the way into life. It was a tragic waste that people were scarcely aware of what was in them and around them ; and she felt that 'the relevance of "art" . . . resides in its power to create, or arouse, and call into operation . . . the human faculty of contemplation.'

In retrospect, the trials and mistakes of her own life

had led up to this new kind of novel she was striving to write. Her ventures and experiments, the struggle to become more alive to other people, were the stuff of her book.

Although every relationship had seen her escaping back to solitude, the state in which she felt most aware, she had also found a sympathy for people that made even near-strangers confide in her, to a singular extent. A letter survives from a young American writer, Frances Gale, doing research in the British Museum Reading Room, who was helped and befriended by Dorothy, and who wrote that Dorothy 'listened with such "alive" silence that I grew garrulous and apologized for it later on, and sinned in the same way at the next opportunity, because something (to this day I don't know what it was) made me want to say things to that girl that I had never even dreamed of trying to tell anyone else.'

Dorothy made another start on her novel, and suddenly it seemed to be working, with 'everything available, all past experience, seen, while I sat writing, for the first time as near, clear, permanent reality.' The novel had begun to be alive, and Miriam existed at its centre, on her own. She, the author, wasn't in it.

She worked on. It was immensely demanding to keep the two visions—hers and Miriam's—apart, and sometimes frustrating, since she only could describe scenes and people as Miriam would register them. Anything familiar to Miriam, that she would only notice obliquely as one does in such cases, would have to be described in the same tangential way. It was 'horrible to refrain from objective description of her family' and other elements of the background.

Miriam was emerging as someone very like what her creator had been, but altered by the fact that it was twenty-two years later; and that girl and those incidents were changed by the action of time. The book, to be true to reality, must illustrate that nothing stood still or was dead and fixed. Virginia Woolf, writing later of *Pilgrimage*, would say: 'An artist tells us that the heart is not, as we should like it to be, a stationary body, but a body which moves perpetually, and is thus always standing in a new relationship to the emotions which are the same.'

Dorothy Richardson would not embroider or consciously dramatize reality. Imagination, to her, was something different from fancy or the creation of extravagant incident. It was the power of creative sympathy, of entering the world of different people, of becoming almost part of things seen and of incidents. It was a spiritual quality, something like love.

The writing itself, the author's style, was a means to an end, and should be simple and translucent like the method itself. Dorothy Richardson's prose was uncommonly simple for its time. We open the first volume, *Pointed Roofs*, to find plain sentences, alight with their simplicity, carrying us along in the being of a young girl about to leave home and go to Germany.

In those first sentences and pages of *Pointed Roofs*— sounding a voice new and different from any that had ever before been heard in literature—there is also an underlying quality of sadness. *Pilgrimage* is a sad book, despite the occasional transcendent joys in it. It is bound to be, since it is a realistic novel, told through a character minutely sensitive to all the misunderstandings, obtuseness and cruelty that people routinely inflict on one another. This vision is perfectly sustained in *Pointed Roofs*, through the clarity of a girl's consciousness at the very outset of her life.

The manuscript of *Pointed Roofs*, completed, would have lain in a drawer. Since it was written in this personal vein, she had 'realized the impossibility of publication'. But Beresford read it, saw its quality, and sent it to a publisher. When it was turned down by this (unspecified) publisher, Dorothy 'hid the returned MS. in a trunk', but Beresford persuaded her to let him send it to Duckworth, whose reader Edward Garnett liked it, classifying it as 'feminine impressionism'; and so it was accepted. She had wanted it to be published under the title of *Pilgrimage*, but 'the covering title being at the moment in use elsewhere, it was issued as *Pointed Roofs*'.

Kate's family at Long Ditton were impressed and

astonished by the news, but not more than Dorothy herself. Beatrice Beresford, a generous, excitable woman, danced round her with joy when the letter came from Duckworth. She predicted a fortune and a motor-car for Dorothy. Dorothy herself felt 'the sense of a heavy burden descending' upon her.

She returned to London. The war had begun, and its disintegrating effect was being felt in society at home. It was a time of exaggerated patriotic fervour, but also of violent reactions against the waste and the sacrifice, and the horrors of the trenches. The desperate hedonism of soldiers home on leave was mirrored in the feverish life of the music halls they frequented, and in the bohemian world, in which the hangers-on of artists, as well as the artists themselves, were living in a decadence recalling the *Yellow Book* nineties, but more bitter and extreme. The safe pre-war world seemed totally gone ; and even warfare had taken on a new horror, with poison gas in the trenches, and air-raids over London itself.

Pointed Roofs was published in the autumn of 1915. Duckworth advertised it as 'A First Novel of Unusual Merit'. The critics were impressed but hostile. *The Saturday Review*, whose editors had been among the first to encourage Dorothy to write a novel, reviewed it under the heading 'An Original Book'. But 'originality ventures into strange lands', wrote the anonymous reviewer, describing the book as 'fictional pathology' and 'a charted dissection of an unsound mind. It lays bare the workings of a sick imagination.' It was early days for writing like this. The book was ahead of its time, both in its way of portraying consciousness, and in the fact that that consciousness was a woman's. Joyce had not yet published *A Portrait of the Artist as a Young Man* and had only just begun writing *Ulysses* ; and *Du Côté de chez Swann*, Proust's first volume of *A la recherche du temps perdu*, had been published in France less than two years before.

The outcome of the Suffragette movement was also in the balance. Public feeling ran high on both sides ; and into the midst of the storm had come this novel portraying an emancipated girl's rebellion against a man's world—a rebellion that, because it was a youthful one, sometimes excessively belittled men's capabilities and faculties. The timing of the book's publication was doubly unfortunate because of the war and anti-German feeling. As *The Times Literary Supplement* reviewer pointed out, 'An exact chronicle of life in a German girls' school a quarter of a century ago . . . is perhaps of all themes which a novelist might choose the least likely to appeal to the public at the present moment'. He also noted, however, that 'Miss Richardson has a special realistic method of identifying herself with her heroine and recording intimate and small details as they affected her, which is vivid and telling'.

It was a new and therefore difficult voice. As Virginia Woolf was to say : 'She has invented or, if she has not invented, developed and applied to her own uses, a sentence which we might call the psychological sentence of the feminine gender.' She had not compromised, by making the reading easier with padding or exposition. Even her punctuation, in the first edition, added to the difficulty. By usual standards she tended to punctuate too little, so as not to break the flow of a sentence, where she felt that to do so would impair its meaning.

However, despite these doubtful and puzzled reactions, the book generally impressed people as a work of importance, both in its viewpoint and in its finely attuned method of registering perception and experience. But for general readers, to whom such a method was entirely new, and who had not yet been trained in intuitive, imaginative reading by her successors Joyce, Virginia Woolf and the rest, it was surprisingly difficult to grasp. So the book was a *succès d'estime*, but sold only moderately. She made very little money from it, not the fortune predicted by Mrs. Beresford.

On returning to London, she had settled again in St. John's Wood. She liked the district with its air of seclusion and its avenue of trees, its 'rabbit-warreny decrepitude' and 'old-world dignity'. Queen's Terrace, a small D-shaped turning off the Finchley Road, was lined with Regency and early-Victorian houses, four-storeyed, narrow but well-proportioned : reminiscent, on a smaller scale, of Endsleigh

Street, and equally dilapidated—the sort of shabby old house, somewhat battered and begrimed but with the remnants of fine plasterwork and ironwork and good marble fireplaces, that made her feel at home. At 32 Queen's Terrace, in the more secluded stretch of the road, out of sight and sound of Finchley Road traffic, she took a top-floor room.

On the floor below, in the seedy grandeur of what had been the old drawing-room, lived a young artist called Alan Odle. The landlady told her confidentially that he was a nice enough young gentleman, courteous and quiet : 'Couldn't have a nicer gentleman in the house, never came home until the small hours, and was sober only during his working day.' He led a wild life with his artist friends, and stayed out drinking half the night in such bohemian West End places as the Café Royal and the Crab Tree Tavern. He hardly ever appeared in the basement dining-room where the landlady served breakfast to her lodgers.

Still, Dorothy did see him occasionally in the dining-room, and also on the stairs. His shabby, even tattered clothes, baggy trousers and threadbare smoking jacket, sagged on his pathetically thin frame ; and his only shoes were cracked patent pumps with the soles flapping loose. His long face, worn-looking and hungry, was lit by the intelligent expression of his fine dark-brown eyes, but he looked sad and lost. His bearing had the over-precise, over-controlled quality of someone who is a heavy drinker but just manages to keep his dignity and equilibrium. His longish hair was swirled back from his face in a futile attempt to keep it in order. In spite of all this, he had an air of immense grandeur. At an art exhibition, someone was heard to say of him : 'Who is that man who's dressed like a dustman and carries himself like a duke ?'

Dorothy was now working on *Backwater*, the second volume of the cycle, carrying on Miriam's experiences to a school in 'Banbury Park' in North London (an ordinary setting to inspire one critic's reaction to the book that 'the exotic seed of the Brontës is producing extraordinary fruit'). She wrote on, despite the noise of building works opposite, where the War Office had torn down a section of the houses, and was replacing them with a large barracks.

She lived very quietly now, and saw very few people. Veronica was occupied with her two children, David, born in 1908, and Rachel. Benjamin was in the Home Guard on sentry duty most nights at the Blackwall Tunnel. Of Kate's family, Dorothy occasionally saw Philip Batchelor, training as an engineer, who had bought himself a motor-cycle to get up to London. Kate's younger child, a girl, had been drowned some years before. It had been a hard blow for Kate and for Batchelor, who had been especially devoted to his daughter.

Early in 1917, the barracks in Queen's Terrace being completed, the King, Queen Mary and their young daughter came in state one morning to open the new building. There was great excitement in Queen's Terrace, the inevitable small crowd collecting to see the royal carriage drive in. The landlady at 32 excitedly knocked at Dorothy's door; she must come down and see the King, Queen and Princess; and the best vantage-point would be the long windows of the old drawing-room below, that 'weird Mr. Odle's' room. Reluctantly Dorothy allowed herself to be taken downstairs. Mr. Odle was out, and the landlady assured her that he wouldn't mind this temporary invasion; but Dorothy was embarrassed.

As they entered his room, the first thing she noticed 'just inside the door', was the quantity of drawings, most of them stacked against the walls. They were extraordinary works, and she couldn't stop looking at them. She was 'knocked sideways' by them, by their 'swift vigour, beauty—and humour'. They showed the influence of Hogarth and of Beardsley, but they had a 'kinetic power' of their own, with their strange elongations and distortions of figures, their bleakness and earthiness, and use of the stark contrast of black and white. They were surprisingly powerful works to have been done by that lost-looking young man.

On a morning shortly afterwards, Odle appeared in the basement for breakfast looking pale and unwell. Dorothy started to talk to him, but there was little response. ('This old hag,' he said later to his brother and sister-in-law, 'comes down to breakfast and tries to make me talk when I haven't been to bed yet.')

She seemed an old hag to a young man like Odle. She was forty-three, and her beauty was gone, together with the slenderness that she had kept through her thirties. Looking back on her youth, she regretted the waste of so much of it in drudgery; although she couldn't recall a time when she hadn't been in love, 'save for brief intervals, from adolescence onwards'. She had lost Wells's child, and discovered her own maternal feelings too late. She would have to content herself with other women's children; and it seemed unlikely that she would marry now. Her family and friends were dispersed, dead, or placed in their own separate lives. She was more on her own than ever before, in this Queen's Terrace backwater.

All she had was her writing, confirmed as the vocation of her life; but she wished she had made something more of her personal life. 'Without people, the first having been one's little lonely self', what could anything matter? She had come a long way from her earlier view of the futility of personal relationships. She envied those people who had 'the blessed ability to say "we" instead of "I"'.

Sometimes, wakeful late at night, she would hear Alan Odle coming quietly home around dawn, and from his room below hers pitiful noises of gasping and choking, as he coughed blood.

These were tubercular attacks, the cause of his thinness and pallor. It was suicidal for a man in his state of health to drink so much, eat so little and keep such late hours. She didn't yet know that he found it 'impossible to get through a day' without drinking heavily. He was one of the young bohemians reacting against the senseless slaughter of the war, and against the conventions of a dying society that had brought about such a state of affairs. These young artists and writers seemed, almost as a duty, to be burning themselves out, escaping from a world they couldn't bear in drink or other excesses.

His younger brother Vincent and Vincent's wife Rose, to

whom he gave accounts of his life at Queen's Terrace, were living not far off in a studio in Abercorn Place. Vincent was an aspiring writer and actor, Rose a teacher of Russian-Jewish parentage, and they had two small children. They noted how Alan was beginning to mention 'Miss Richardson' more and more often ; and then to quote her views, and to tell them admiringly how she had managed to live on next to nothing, in order to be free to write her books.

That first reluctant exchange of politenesses in the basement at Queen's Terrace had developed into friendship. He had always cared more for books than for eating, 'having absorbed, in starveling student days, the whole of the classics' ; and he took to sharing her breakfast table and 'discoursing with eighteenth-century formality' on literature.

She discovered that the strength she had seen in his drawings was part of his character too. Despite his illness and his drinking, he continued to work, both on his own drawings and on the art work for the magazine *The Gypsy*, which included among its contributors Eden Phillpotts, Edmund Gosse and Israel Zangwill. *The Times*, in its review of a 1915 edition, had noted 'this violent and various Mr. Alan Odle, who flings his riotous brutalities so hotly upon so many of its pages'.

She found that he was hopeless at looking after himself, 'helpless in all the affairs of life', and he wouldn't eat properly. Touched by his plight and protective by nature, and finding she now had some influence over him, she tried to make him take better care of himself, though she still 'had no idea . . . of the completeness of his dependence on drink'. Spending more time with her, he was less often out all night drinking with his cronies. She met some of these, and a few became her friends as well : in particular Henry Savage, *The Gypsy*'s literary editor, and Adrian Allinson, a portrait painter who was always in difficulties with an endless succession of girl friends. These people belonged to a set frequenting certain literary and artistic salons, and various haunts from the Café Royal to the more ordinary Fleming's Restaurant in Oxford Street, a place that Dorothy already knew and liked for its lively but unpretentious atmosphere.

However, she didn't altogether fit in with his friends, who resented her steadying effect on him. Savage denounced her one evening as 'unworthy to enter a pub'.

Alan was converted to her habit of walking round London, and talking absorbedly on these long walks. The next volume of *Pilgrimage*, *The Tunnel*, would describe Miriam's early days in Bloomsbury; and with Alan replacing Benjamin Grad, Dorothy was covering the ground of twenty years before. London still endlessly fascinated her.

If Alan was moving away from the influence of his wild companions, it was his choice. Dorothy's company helped him to get through the days without drinking so heavily. He seemed less unhappy and less cynical. He happened on the notes of that nonsense news sheet she had compiled years before with her friend Winifred Ray. It so amused him that he approached a Fleet Street acquaintance with a view to getting it published as 'D.T.'s Weekly'. The journalist was interested, but the paper shortage put an end to the project.

Rose and Vincent Odle grew impatient to meet Miss Richardson, about whom they were hearing so much. So a meeting was arranged. The four were to dine one evening at Fleming's, 'to the music of Strauss and the voices of the circumambient typists ... in the uttermost basement'. Rose Odle, still a teacher, was held up that day at her school and had to rush to the restaurant, after settling her children with the woman who was minding them.

Hurrying had made her so hot that, arriving at Fleming's, she went into the cloakroom, plunged her head in the basin, and ran the cold water tap over it. She wore her hair short, and as she quickly rubbed it dry, it curled round her head in a casual fashion. As she came to the table where the others were waiting, the first thing she noticed about Dorothy was her magnificent golden hair, wound round her head, in contrast to her own mass of curls.

To Rose, a generation younger, Dorothy, who had been such a rebel in her youth, now looked like an almost Establishment figure of dignity and conventionality—

until the talk moved on to controversial topics, and Dorothy showed that she was still an individual thinker.

She and Rose had much in common. Rose too had broken away from her family, leaving home in her teens to get away from an unbalanced stepfather, becoming a socialist and a member of the Fabian Society nursery, where she had once dared to argue with Shaw. She had joined a dramatic society, where she met Vincent Odle, two years younger than herself, a tall, pale, romantically handsome young man with a Grecian profile. Almost at once he had fallen in love with her. She was less sure at first, but finally she had accepted his proposal. They had married despite the disapproval of both their families.

Samuel Odle, the father of Alan and Vincent and another, older brother, was a retired bank manager in Sittingbourne, Kent. He was an excessively proper and conventional man, and hearing of Vincent's entanglement with 'an older woman', an 'adventuress', had stormed up to London, only to find that he was just too late to stop them from marrying; but before long he accepted the match with a fairly good grace.

Rose's mother was a brave and remarkable woman who had fled, as a young widow, from the Kiev pogroms, and arriving in London had struggled to qualify as a nurse and raise her three children. As a Charity nurse, she had been on call night and day, working mainly among the East End poor; but, for all her compassion, she couldn't forgive her daughter's marriage to a gentile, one of the persecuting race who had murdered her first husband and driven her to escape with her children from Russia.

The talk, this first evening at Fleming's, became more and more lively, ranging over books, films, politics and social questions. The ice between the four was soon broken; and walking home afterwards, Rose and Vincent speculated on how serious was the involvement between Alan and Dorothy, despite the disparity in their ages.

In fact, Alan was about to ask Dorothy to marry him. It was a momentous step for him. At twenty-eight, his wrecked health had made him essentially withdrawn, solitary, courteously self-contained and cynical, though his 'cynicism was never very deeply corrosive'. He had lived almost entirely among men—his widower father and two brothers, and his cronies at *The Gypsy* and elsewhere in Soho—and he knew little of women, and tended to avoid them out of mistrust of their poses. When he met Veronica Grad, he didn't take to her greatly, even though she liked him and was charming to him. Her undoubted intelligence and grace couldn't reconcile him to her feminine artifice.

Dorothy, who had always been a champion of women's values (more than women's rights), had moved on from her earlier attitude of overstating the case of women and underestimating men. ('It was our mutual dislike of the sex-as-a-whole [women] that first drew Alan and me together,' she wrote subsequently.) In spite of her feminism—even from the start, in her relationship with her father, for all their disputes—she had been a man's woman. Her closest involvements, apart from Veronica, had been with men ; and in living with women she had seen the pettiness and un-reason that were often part of their closeness to life—although she believed that it was a man's world, restricting and narrowing women, that made them like this. Tending to like men better than women, she had always had the power to attract men around her; the Endsleigh Street lodgers, her Harley Street friends, the Quaker farmer Penrose who had taken her on those marketing trips through the Sussex coast towns, and mostly lately, a new admirer, Josiah Wedgwood, the radical M.P.

Wedgwood wrote in his autobiography that in 'the autumn of 1916 . . . I first came to hear of Zionism as a creed, through . . . Dorothy Richardson, and her friend . . . who got me to address a meeting of the elect'. The friend, whom Wedgwood calls 'Berg', was almost certainly Benjamin Grad. Wedgwood became a keen supporter of this cause, and was one of the prime movers behind the Balfour Declaration of 1917, giving the support of the British Government to the establishment in Palestine of a national home for the Jewish people.

Alan occupied Dorothy more and more. In the last year

or two, his health had worsened, through bad attacks of 'flu, which she had caught as well. More often confined to his room at Queen's Terrace, he had grown increasingly dependent on her. He was totally unworldly and impractical, unable to deal with the simplest necessities of food, clothing, money, forgetful of everything apart from his work and the people he cared for.

He also had great charm and presence, a sweetness of manner, and a generous nature. His face was attractive and expressive with its handsome brown eyes. Dorothy cared for him deeply—but not enough to marry him.

After she had refused him, they still saw each other continually. She learned more about his family and his past life. His father, the bank manager of Sittingbourne, whose only passion outside business was cricket, was so unimaginative a man that it was the height of irony that of his three sons the eldest, Sidney, had wanted to be a musician, the second, Alan, was an artist, and the youngest, Vincent, became a writer. Of the three, Alan had reacted most completely against the stifling home environment. Sidney had proved the most malleable, distinguishing himself as a local cricketer and giving up his music—only to be driven into a breakdown.

By great good fortune, a well-to-do client at the bank, a retired Customs officer whose bank balance Mr. Odle respected, had chanced to see some of Alan's youthful drawings, had been impressed by them, and had told Mr. Odle that a talent like this could be turned to good account. Thanks to this sponsor, Alan was enabled to attend classes at the Sidney-Cooper Art School in Canterbury, where his individual bent showed itself early, and his mannered but powerful style developed quickly.

In the atmosphere of the art world he let his appearance go, and he grew his hair longer; but reports of his progress were encouraging enough, for Mr. Odle grudgingly to allow him to go on up to London, to continue his studies at the St. John's Wood Art School.

His occasional letters to his father, addressed to the bank and sometimes franked with a drawing of a conspicuously naked cherub, infuriated Mr. Odle. He was making his son a small allowance, on which Alan, impractical as he was, couldn't manage to eat properly; and so his health suffered. When his father asked him what he would do if his allowance were stopped, he replied simply: 'I'd starve.' He had been working in the hope of an exhibition; but so far he had not achieved one. The war curtailed such possibilities.

In 1917, soon after his proposal to Dorothy, he was called up before an Army Selection Board and inducted into the Army—for a day. One of the N.C.O.s noticed how ill he looked, and he was sent to a specialist for a proper examination. They invalided him out on the spot, telling him his tuberculosis was so far advanced that he might have six months to live; though rest and a change of air and diet might give him somewhat longer.

Back at Queen's Terrace, he told Dorothy what had happened. Dorothy, about to go down to Cornwall to the Beresfords, stayed on in London to be with him. Recovering from his first shock, he resolutely started work again, and she travelled down to Cornwall.

Again he had pressed her to marry him, and this time she had nearly consented. She was moved by his plight, but compassion had seemed to her not the right motive for marriage between two essentially solitary people.

In Cornwall she continued to be preoccupied with Alan and his trouble. At a distance she realized how fond of him she was and how close they had become. They wrote to each other, oddly formal little notes: his beautifully set out in his engraved way of writing, little works of art; hers, in her fine, somewhat mediaeval hand, scarcely less so. (Another friend once said, of a letter from her: 'What a thing it is to *look at*, even.')

This surface formality, together with certain little set jokes that she and Alan had, like the new, slightly bitter one of her calling him by the nickname 'Sergeant' in commemoration of his one day in the Army—these were their protection against too intense an involvement with each other. Both were afraid of any very deep commitment. These safety devices allowed them to keep their relationship

66

on an easy footing; and that was what finally swung the balance. She agreed to marry him.

It seemed that she was not risking much, since the doctors had given him six months to live. But at least she could see him through that time.

Having promised to marry him, she journeyed up to London from Cornwall. Twice on the train she lost her nerve and got off, but each time she changed her mind again, and went on up to London.

29 August was fixed as the day for the marriage. Alan decided to keep it a secret from his father for the moment, in case Mr. Odle should stop his small allowance. He would presently be too ill to work, and already he and Dorothy between them had barely enough to keep themselves even in poverty. His brother Vincent and Rose were asked to keep the secret.

Mr. Odle in the intervening years had re-married, and later moved to Tunbridge Wells. His new wife had been housekeeper to Alan's patron the Customs officer, now dead. She had had financial expectations on the death of her employer, but these had been only partially fulfilled. Mr. Odle, having made up his mind that she would be a useful wife to look after him in his declining years, had postponed their marriage until after his retirement. His reason had been this. If he married her before he retired, then she would be entitled to a pension from the bank when he died; but as it was, with no pension due to her, it would be in her best interest to look after him devotedly, since her support from him would end with his death, apart from any sum that he might or might not choose to leave her.

As for Dorothy's finances, her reputation continued to grow, but not yet the sales of her books; though later Duckworth began to pay her a small annual sum, an advance on future royalties. Meanwhile she had received an advance of £15 each, for the second and third volumes of *Pilgrimage*.

The Times Literary Supplement, reviewing *Honeycomb* in the autumn of 1917, commented that 'the uneven surface is the surface of Miriam's being . . . with its aspirations and checks and dashes out to life; and, tiresome though it often is, the book holds our interest close to a young person who is intensely and independently "alive" . . . The book succeeds, through the author's intensity of feeling and thought, in conveying (in defiance of all the laws of good writing) a clear impression of the girl and of the society [around her]'. *The Saturday Review*, in its notice of *Honeycomb*, referred as before to her 'morbid and self-conscious mind' and 'the talent of neurasthenia'. 'She must learn,' said the reviewer, again an anonymous one, 'that health is essential to literature'. But he referred grudgingly to her 'considerable gifts'. Similarly the *Spectator*, having ignored the three earlier volumes, in the following year printed a notice of *The Tunnel* by a critic who described himself, with querulous puzzlement over the book, as an 'elderly male reviewer', and complained that 'we are spared few of the menial and even loathsome details of her calling', referring to Miriam's work as a dental secretary. As a judgment against *Pilgrimage*, he noted that 'it is like watching a cinema show' ; and he commented with disfavour on the fact that 'in no modern novel has the method of translating unuttered thoughts been carried so far'.

In this way, critics by and large were attacking *Pilgrimage* for the very qualities of poetic realism which her great contemporaries and successors were developing, and to which the reading public was gradually learning to respond. Joyce, Virginia Woolf and others would fare better at the hands of the critics. Dorothy Richardson had drawn the first critical fire, and the attacks on her work as 'sordid' and 'difficult' have continued to mark her reputation to this day.

In France, where the successive volumes of Proust's novel were published, keeping pace with hers, a few people noted the parallel between the two works, though one of these novels was very English in its underlying seriousness, its concern with ideas and issues as well as experience, the other quintessentially French in its sublime trivialities. One French critic later described Dorothy Richardson's work as 'proustienne avant Proust'.

It occurred to Dorothy, as the day of her marriage to Alan approached, that dearly though they loved St. John's

Wood and all their London background, she must try to take him away from here, where there were too many associations of an old separate life. The pull might be too strong for them both—for him back to his Café Royal set, and to drinking to forget his coming death, and for her to the habit of solitude. Whether or not he lived for more than six months, she resolved that their marriage should not be a failure. But there were 'misgivings on both sides'. 'If I had had the remotest inkling,' she wrote later, 'of the possibility of his surviving me, I would never have consented to marry him.'

The day of their marriage was chilly for August—more like a late autumn day, with gusting showers and a sharp wind rising to 'the force of half a gale'. The Grads did not come to the wedding at the St. Marylebone Register Office; they had bought the ring, since Alan had not had the money to pay for it.

On the marriage certificate, Dorothy's age was given as thirty-seven, seven years less than her true age—a rather endearing feminine deceit, and unthinkable in the austere girl that she had been in her youth. It signalled her intention to live in a less committed way, and become like other ordinary women : for her a 'whole new world . . . possessing its own trials and difficulties and complexities'.

In 'risking the adventure', in going this way, she was endangering something that had grown up in solitude and absolute commitment, and that might not survive in this new way of life. What she was risking was, simply, her genius.

Pointed Roofs was written in 1913 when Dorothy Richardson was forty, in the converted chapel lent her by the Beresfords in St. Ives. To Beresford's amusement and dismay, she had written the manuscript on a 'weird assortment' of papers. 'Half superstitiously afraid of methodical niceties', she declined to have everything neatly laid out for her writing, or use the Roget's *Thesaurus* he offered her, lest the writing should come out too lifelessly precise. Nor did she ever use the press-cutting album that Beresford gave her.

She had been completely absorbed in the novel, living as a recluse while she wrote it, scarcely bothering to eat. Exhausted physically and mentally by the effort, she found herself at the same time replenished by this 'state of intense concentration'.

The book itself, re-creating and clarifying the past of twenty-two years before, stayed close to its original. Dorothy became Miriam; her three sisters she re-named Sarah, Eve and Harriett; the Richardsons were now the Hendersons; incidents and impressions were set down exactly as she recalled them.

But recollection involves certain changes. In this perspective of twenty-two years later, relationships, incidents and people were seen to differ somewhat from what they had seemed to be originally. The pang of this second view, of seeing how often she had erred and been unjust or inadequate, gives these first volumes of *Pilgrimage* an added poignancy, even beyond that conveyed by its sense of youth recaptured.

The mode of writing she adopted, or created, was very well suited to portraying the viewpoint of youth, so subjective and fitful. But it was also her aim, with the successive volumes carrying the story forward over years, to portray Miriam's consciousness changing and developing, from her 'early vagueness' to an 'increasing articulateness', so that at each stage the narrative would take on a slightly altered tone, filtered through the new Miriam who was constantly evolving. To show this change so fully, to dramatize not only the events of someone's life but also the evolution of her consciousness, was a grand design and at that time— since Proust's *A la recherche du temps perdu* was still unpublished—an unprecedented one.

Her method, necessarily omitting whatever would not come into Miriam's own consciousness, also left out much of what she regarded as the dead material, the padding of people's lives, the moments of some totally second-hand activity or mechanical exchange of civilities : the moment without awareness. She could be selective in this way, because 'surely what fiction, at its best can do, is to arrange data, truths, in their real relationship by a process of selection'.

It was consciousness that was her subject matter, and she explored it exhaustively. She had rejected the claims of science, as leaving out of the formulae all those things that could not be formulated, but she was still a product of the age of Darwinism, in spite of her rebellion against it ; and what she opposed was, in any case, a 'misrepresented Darwinism'. Her own methods as a novelist were analytic. She was exploring the frontiers between objective and subjective reality, that much disputed territory.

So those moments when consciousness is deadened in some encounter totally unreal in her meaning of reality— these she could leave out. Undoubtedly she was at times too austere in this way ; and her work occasionally suffers from being too compressed, too high-grade a mixture, with too little ordinariness in it ; and sometimes she omits to give us connecting links that we need when a character suddenly appears or reappears in the story.

But in the ordinary realities of life, as opposed to the dead, rote moments, she greatly believed—in the simple task and word and the ordinary domestic routine, and in the fact that 'everyone, every single soul, has all potentialities'. The existence of quite hackneyed objects—a bar of soap, a scrap of linoleum refracting the light—would at times strike her as almost miraculous, harking back to her own childhood wonder that anything at all could exist. To be properly aware of simple everyday things was to her more important than anything the intellect could formulate. Her writing makes much of these commonplace things.

Light itself was almost a divinity for her, as for the Impressionist painters to whom her work is so closely related, as is that of Proust, who underlined this affinity by the important rôle that he gave to the Impressionist painter Elstir in his novel.

By the time of her marriage in 1917, Dorothy Richardson had completed three chapter-volumes of *Pilgrimage*. Autobiographical as they largely were, reflecting on the facts of her own life, their details are relevant here.

The first volume, *Pointed Roofs*, opens on the eve of Miriam Henderson's journey to Hanover. She is seventeen, and about to leave her beloved home in Barnes to go abroad as a pupil-teacher. Alone in her room which 'would never have its old look again', and then with her sisters, Sarah, Eve and Harriett, and their parents, she is in a turmoil of recollections, expectations, regrets at the end of her schooldays, of 'silent sunny mornings with all the day ahead and nothing to do and no end anywhere to anything; no more sitting at the open window in the dining-room, reading Lecky and Darwin and bound *Contemporary Reviews* with roses waiting in the garden to be worn in the afternoon, and Eve and Harriett somewhere about, washing blouses or copying waltzes from the library packet . . . no more Harriett looking in at the end of the morning, rushing her off to the new grand piano to play the *Mikado* and the *Holy Family* duets. The tennis-club would go on, but she would not be there.'

As for her friend Ted Burton, the counterpart of Dorothy's own suitor in Barnes, 'Why had he come to tea every Sunday—never missing a single Sunday—all the winter? Why did he say: "Play *Abide with me*", "Play *Abide with me*", yesterday, if he didn't care? What was the good of being so quiet and saying nothing? Why didn't he say:

"Don't go?" or : "When are you coming back?"? Eve said he looked perfectly miserable ... There was nothing to look forward to now but governessing and old age.'

She awakes the next morning, the morning of her departure, from a dream of failure and misery at the German school. In the dream the staff had come 'and stood and looked at her, and saw her as she was, without courage, without funds or good clothes or beauty, without charm or interest, without even the skill to play a part ... They would be so affable at first. She had been through it a million times—all her life—all eternity. They would smile those hateful women's smiles—smirks—self-satisfied smiles as if everybody were agreed about everything.'

Accompanied by her father, she makes the crossing to Holland, where he characteristically tries to impress the Dutch porter by letting him think she is going as a pupil to a finishing school. All the same, she finds her father touching. 'There could be no doubt that he was playing the rôle of the English gentleman. Poor dear. It was what he had always wanted to be. He had sacrificed everything to the idea.' But, to his justification : 'No one else's father went with a party of scientific men "for the advancement of science" to Norway or America, seeing the Falls and Yosemite Valley. No one else took his children as far as Dawlish for the holidays, travelling all day, from eight till seven ... no esplanade, the old stone jetty and coves and cowrie shells.' This is all very like Charles Richardson, who had similarly gone to America in 1888 on a British Association conference. His social climbing was as it is described here in *Pilgrimage*, and the details of family summer holidays are those of Dorothy's own childhood : she even mentioned the cowrie shells at Dawlish in one of her letters.

The account of Miriam's life at Fräulein Pfaff's (Fräulein Pabst's) school in Hanover throws light on Dorothy's own experience as a pupil-teacher. Miriam settles uneasily into the ways of the school, with its tightly strung atmosphere. Gradually a vivid picture is built up of Fräulein herself, with her 'clear profile, the sallow, hollow cheeks, the

73

same heavy bonyness that Anna the servant had, but finer and redeemed by the wide eye that was so strange . . . the quick youthfulness of those steady eyes', and her changing moods, alternately charming, domineering, sentimental.

Miriam's first evening at the school is a musical evening, and the playing transforms her 'English ideas of music'. But some weeks later, when the others hear her playing the *Sonata Pathétique*, they are astonished that an English girl can play like this, and Fräulein calls her a 'real musician'. However, she is always insecure and self-conscious, a 'misanthrope', 'not like other people'. Her unsureness and self-dislike are a projection of Dorothy's own, at that time of her life.

Gradually Miriam finds that she can teach; and she has got over her first homesickness. But the teaching of the German masters disappoints her: they have a pompous reverence for the facts, but 'the relationship of their pupils to those facts seemed a matter of less than indifference to them'.

The atmosphere of Germany encloses and moves her, more 'even than the old first house she had kissed the morning they came away—the flower-filled garden, the river, the woods'. She who had been an agnostic, even finds something in the church service here that there had not been in England: 'They were singing a hymn . . . There was time for Miriam to read the first line and recognize the original of "Now thank we all our God" before the singing had reached the third syllable. She hung over the book, "Nun-dank-et-al-le-Gott." Now-thank-all-God. She read that first line again and felt how much better the thing was without the "we" and the "our". What a perfect phrase . . . The hymn rolled on and she recognized that it was the tune she knew—the hard square tune she and Eve had called it—and Harriett used to mark time to it in jerks, a jerk to each syllable, with a twisted glove-finger tip just under the book ledge with her left hand, towards Miriam. But sung as these Germans sung it, it did not jerk at all. It did not sound like a "proclamation" or an order. It was . . . somehow . . . everyday. The notes seemed to hold her up. This was—Luther—Germany—the Reforma-

tion—solid and quiet. She glanced up and then hung more
closely over her book. It was the stained-glass windows
that made the Schloss Kirche so dark. One movement of her
head showed her that all the windows within sight were
dark with rich colour, and there was oak everywhere—
great shelves and galleries and juttings of dark wood, great
carved masses and a high dim roof and strange spaces of
light . . . "Nun danket alle Gott". There was nothing to
object to in that. Everybody could say that . . . Emma and
Clara were chanting on either side of her. Immediately
behind her sounded the quavering voice of an old woman.
They all felt it. She must remember that . . . Think of it
every day.'

There are escapades, factions, outings, long country
walks. She lets herself go on the evening of the school
charades. 'People always liked her if she let herself go.' But
distressingly she witnesses Fräulein Pfaff's hysteria, directed
first against the French master and then in a screaming
match with the maid. When the French master starts to
take an interest in Miriam, Fräulein, who regards him as her
property, is jealous. Afterwards she is often sarcastic with
Miriam, though occasionally showing her kindness and
warmth.

Throughout the narrative Dorothy refers, with only slight
changes, to the reactions and events of her own childhood,
from those earliest memories in Abingdon (called Babington
in the novel) to 'one of waking up on her seventh birthday
in the seaside villa alone in a small dark room . . . and, after
a curious moment when the darkness seemed to move
against her, feeling very old and crying bitterly'. The
recollections of life in Barnes re-create the known circumstances of Dorothy's own life. She refers to her father's
financial troubles, and her anxiety for her mother; and her
parents' relationship is clearly set out, with her father's
patronizing 'remarks about the gullibility of women' and
his 'neighing laugh' at her mother that 'had come again
and again all through the years until she sat meekly, flushed
and suffering under the fierce gaslight'. But after his financial
crash, when they are living in reduced circumstances in the

Gunnersbury villa lent them by Sarah's husband (just as Dorothy's brother-in-law Arthur Batchelor had given up his home to the Richardsons), Miriam overhears a moment of touching rapprochement between her parents: 'Her father and mother, whose failure and death she had foreseen as a child with sudden bitter tears, were now going on step by step towards these ghostly things in the small bright lamplit villa . . . They had some secret together and did not feel the darkness. Their eyes were careless and bright. Startled, she had heard them laugh together as they talked in their room.'

The moral and intellectual dilemmas of Dorothy's own youth, the 'early secret worries' over free will and religion, her stubbornness and awkwardness, and also her sense of wonder 'to excess': all these elements are reproduced in Miriam's consciousness. Towards the end of the term, Fräulein tells her that she has a vocation for teaching, but that she must conquer her unfortunate manner, her chill formality and stiffness. Fräulein is a person who must make her effect by breaking one down. Miriam knows that she herself cannot keep up an act, and seem to be like other people, and 'charming'.

Miriam now has a letter from Eve telling her of Harriett's engagement. Harriett, her youngest and favourite sister, amusing and bright, is totally undaunted and unchanged by the family's misfortunes. Her engagement to Gerald, as Eve relates the details—'regularly in the seat behind us at All Saints' for months . . . made up his mind then—the moment he saw her . . . made a solemn call—*admirably* suited to each other—rather a long melancholy good-looking face— they look such a contrast . . . not exactly a clerk—something rather above that, to do with making drafts of things and so on'—refers us back to Jessie Richardson and Jack Hale, who were married in that same church of All Saints' on Barnes Common, and whose subsequent vicissitudes and moves were, by Jessie Hale's own account, accurately reflected in *Pilgrimage*.

The letter from Eve also summons Miriam home. The end of her six months in Germany sees her, like her creator before her, having those complicated reactions of regret and relief that made it impossible for Dorothy Richardson, through much of her life, to commit herself freely to any one situation or person. One close friend had 'the impression that Dorothy was always somewhat withdrawn, afraid for long years . . . to give herself completely. There was always a *noli me tangere* about her : too great a friendship might mean a parallel loss.'

Miriam is always aware of the duality of people, including herself ; and there is an ironic aptness in Fräulein's last word on her on the station platform at Hanover : 'You and I have, I think, much in common.' Miriam, or 'Dorothy-Miriam', as a writer friend would later refer to Dorothy, is as changeable and moody, and as powerful a character, as Fräulein herself.

The setting of *Backwater* (published 1916) is the Banbury Park school of the Misses Perne, where Miriam is now to teach, as Dorothy had taught at the Misses Ayre's school in the Finsbury/Barnsbury Park district of North London. From the beginning she finds the district antipathetic with its mean streets and 'hard intent faces . . . the harsh snarling monotone of the North London voice'.

But the eldest Miss Perne is as charming as her original, Miss Ayre. She is described as being 'very tall . . . with a delicate wrinkled creamy face and coal-black eyes' and black hair like Miss Ayre's. The middle sister, Miss Jennie, is the talkative, lively one ; and the youngest, Miss Haddie, 'with neat smooth green-grey hair and a long, sad greyish face and faded eyes', is devoutly religious and becomes earnestly interested in Miriam's spiritual welfare.

Miriam's suitor Ted Burton is coming to the Hendersons' dance tomorrow evening ; and she is determined to respond to him this time, instead of turning to stone when he speaks her name in that urgent way. But as she tries to think of him, his image recedes into darkness. 'That darkness was dreadful. It was his own life. She would never know it. However well they got to know each other, they would always be strangers.'

77

This refers back to Dorothy's own turning-point at Barnes, when, having lived away from that world for a time, she found it too confined and yet also more attractive than ever, a kind of paradise lost: which is another recurrent theme of *Pilgrimage*, as Miriam is time and again drawn to people and milieux that are not suitable for her, but remind her of her sheltered life in Barnes before the family's fall from grace; so that on the social level too, her Pilgrimage is a journey towards redemption.

On the morning of the party, with the changeableness of youth, she feels happy, smokes her first cigarette and is intoxicated with it. That evening, playing the piano for the dancers, she is troubled by Ted's lateness: 'Why did he not come? Presently she would be cold and sick and done for, for the evening.' As soon as he arrives, he comes straight to her, accompanied by a friend she has never met before: an intelligent attractive man, Max, who is Jewish.

She dances first with this Max, to whom she is drawn, and then again with Max—'She had never really danced before'—strangely impelled to put off her first dance with Ted. And then she takes Max out to show him the garden, evading Ted. Max says to her: 'I feel that there is no poison in you. I have not felt that before with a woman.' He asks her to wait a year for him. He is going on business to New York.

Max, a Jew, someone totally outside her own background, more individual than Ted, and therefore attractive to her, is the forerunner of Benjamin Grad in Dorothy's own life. Max too, for all his businessman's toughness, has a certain vulnerability, being a Jew and an outsider; and this vulnerable quality appeals to Miriam. With men like this, it is easier to have a relationship of equals, rather than the subservient one of most Victorian women. Dorothy, with the forceful, overweening character that often goes with genius, was drawn to people needing protection, who would lean on her.

When an Irish pupil-teacher, Julia Doyle, is engaged by the Pernes, Miriam, who is normally so shy with strangers, is surprisingly eager to meet the girl's train at Liverpool

Street station. At first Julia treats her as a mentor, but by the following term is starting to encroach on Miriam's own responsibilities, always with a seeming concern for the elder girl's tiredness. Subtly conveyed is Julia's hidden, half-unconscious resentment of Miriam, who, seeing these complexities, is no match for someone acting on a much simpler level.

These subtle betrayals are frequent in *Pilgrimage*, providing another undercurrent of tension in passages that seem on the surface uneventful and quiet. This theme of betrayal harks back to the early days of family uncertainties, that time when nothing was stable or reliable. In the world of *Pilgrimage*, betrayals seem almost inevitable : people are constantly changing and ceasing to be to one what they were before.

Miriam still has no definite aim or direction, and is restless, evading close ties. Miss Haddie Perne, who tries to befriend her, is kept at a distance. Miriam has long solitary walks in the park, and finds another escape, through the penny library, into a new world of forbidden novels, to which she becomes addicted for a time, though they tend to dissolve into 'conversations, discussions, situations, arguments, "fusses"—all about nothing'. She is becoming almost professionally interested in the elements of writing ; and her dissatisfaction with most novels that she reads echoes Dorothy's own. This tendency to escape, and even escapism, is for her a first step towards the artist's creation of his own distinct world.

So far she has cut herself off from her original background, without yet replacing it. She is miserable at returning to Banbury Park for the second term ; but during the holiday people at home have talked 'to you about things that are only theirs now, and not wanting to hear about yours . . . not about the little real everyday things that give you an idea of anything, but only the startling things that are not important'.

She has had the news that Max—for whose sake she let Ted Burton go—has died of influenza in New York. She is troubled, this term, with headaches and exhaustion, and with longings for a fuller sort of life. Reading a popular novel, she relates herself to a character in it, 'one of the bad characters who are turned out of the happy homes. I'm some sort of bad unsimple woman.'

In fact she has succeeded at Banbury Park in being accepted : 'This is the utmost. I've won. There'll never be anything more than this here.' It isn't enough for her. She cannot yet settle for this.

Religion continues to trouble her. She cannot entirely reject it, though mainly aesthetic aspects rather than the ritual move her, as in the service at the Schloss Kirche, and as in Dorothy's own childhood experience of services at the Abingdon church and All Saints' in Barnes. But at a service in the Banbury Park church, where there is nothing aesthetic in the music or architecture, Miriam feels a revulsion : 'What was it all about? . . . Everybody was dying in cold secret fear. Christ, the son of God, was part of it all, the same family . . . vindictive.' When Miss Haddie discovers her doubts, Miriam exclaims to her : 'How can I help it if faith seems to me just an abnormal condition of the mind with fanaticism at one end and agnosticism at the other?'

These are Dorothy's own doubts again, her concern as a girl for 'the apparent irrationality of the Christian faith'. She is looking for a religious belief that will correspond to her more personal moments of illumination. At the Pernes' one day, reading the newspaper has made her doubt her own ability to cope with the tough modern world. 'She would not be wanted.' And then on her way upstairs to her room, she becomes 'aware of a curious buoyancy rising within her' and a joyful sense of her own miraculous aliveness. But 'what's the use of feeling like that if it doesn't stay? . . . There's something in me that can't be touched or altered. Me. If it comes again. If it's stronger every time . . . Perhaps it goes on getting stronger till you die.' But she has not yet found her answer to the problem, just as Dorothy wrote of herself at the corresponding time that 'the mystics, so far' she 'had not encountered' in her struggles with religion.

Grace Broom, a pupil with whom Miriam is friendly,

comes out of a delirium of illness saying she is now certain there is another life. Miriam is excited and moved by the girl's revelation : if 'Grace upstairs in her room' had 'really seen the white light away in the distance far beyond the noise of the world?'

Although Miriam, in the enclosed life of this school, has begun to feel Dorothy's own expressed 'longing to escape from the world of women', still women are more generally attractive to Miriam than men. Her feelings for the Pernes and Grace, and even Julia Doyle, are more emotional than any of her rather insubstantial attachments to young men. She is struck by the courage of most women, and their brightness in a world in which they are the underdog, and yet they manage to exist more intensely than most men. Her mother, for all her instability, has this courage, which she shows now when faced with an operation, though 'things had reached their worst, the house going to be sold, pater and mother and Sarah going into lodgings in September'.

In a brief respite from these troubles, Miriam, wandering alone by the sea, has another moment of transcendent joy, and 'she tried to remember when the strange independent joy had begun, and thought she could trace it back to a morning in the garden at Babington, the first thing she could remember . . . She wanted to speak to someone of these things. Until she could speak to someone about them, she must always be alone'. But so much is disillusioning, including the sly attitudes and glances of men in the street. 'Life was ugly and cruel. The secret of the sea and of the evenings and mornings must be given up. It would fade more and more. What was life? Either playing a part all the time in order to be amongst people in the warm, or standing alone with the strange true real feeling—alone with a sort of edge of reality on everything ; even on quite ugly common things—cheap boarding-houses, face-towels and blistered window frames.'

As her year at the school draws to a close, she is told by the Pernes, distressed to lose her, how successful she has been as a teacher. She knows that 'the business of the teacher is to make the children independent, to get them to think for themselves, and that's much more important than whether they get to know facts'.

In *Honeycomb* (published 1917) the Avorys of Dorothy's own experience as a governess have become the Corries. The comfort and elegance of their home, a large place in the country, reminds her again—though this background is grander—of Barnes.

At times Miriam feels battered and worn by her pillar-to-post existence, and also frightened, as in that moment at the Pernes' when she had suddenly doubted her ability to cope with the modern world. Mrs. Corrie, a charming, social, selfish woman who is adept at using people, urges Miriam to stay with them permanently; and the girl is tempted to accept. In Mrs. Corrie Dorothy Richardson portrays, with the subtlety that marks her characterization of women more than of men, the charm and narrowness and brittle unhappiness of the conventional social woman who yet has some intelligence and awareness that are wasted in that kind of life. Another of these women, Mrs. Kronen, a South African, who is a guest of the Corries, is more ruthless in pursuing social vanities and pleasures, and thereby achieves a more definite character and style than Mrs. Corrie. These women are interesting to Miriam for their ability to create an atmosphere : something about which she will gradually make further discoveries.

Going up to London for the day with Mrs. Corrie, she has half an hour's walk alone for the first time in the West End, and she has a sense of its mystery and power, and of herself as belonging to it. But behind everything nowadays is the disgrace and stigma marking her, because of her father's ruin.

Trying to fix the beauty that she still sees everywhere, she buys a sketch-book and water colours and fills 'sheet after sheet with swift efforts to recall Brighton skies . . . her thoughts of the great brow and downward sweep of cliff and the sea coming up to it was not a picture, it was a thing . . . an experience, perhaps the most important thing in life.'

Felix Corrie, the coldly dispassionate lawyer, shows

another facet of the scientific or professional mentality in men that she finds so limited. Corrie likes her and is impressed by her intelligence, but she finds that 'he can't look at anything from the point of view of life as a whole'. She has a transitory success at a party of the Corries when she is surrounded by the men and plays billiards with them and talks to them as an equal, but then sees that Mrs. Corrie and the other women have ostracized her for it.

So much of the contact between people, as Miriam observes it, is founded in vanity or pretence or mutual exploitation. She looks for a reality in relationships to match the reality of her own awareness of things. But at times she blames herself for finding so much emptiness in people's lives. Perhaps she is too much caught up in herself to understand other people or to care for them deeply. These doubts are the start of an awakening, for her.

The only equal relationship that she has observed between a man and a woman is that of her youngest sister Harriett and Harriett's husband Gerald, who 'liked mouching about and . . . looking for hours in shop windows and strolling on the Heath. Liked bulls-eyes.' But Gerald turns out to be another outsider. His parents, who had lived on a lavish scale in Chelsea, had died when he was young, having spent most of their fortune. Gerald had inherited a small private income and his parents' expensive tastes; and soon he will become dissatisfied with his humdrum job and break away from it, moving with Harriett to Brighton (as Jessie and Jack Hale had moved to Hastings), to run a boarding-house and be free of the office routine.

Escape is, then, a dominant theme not only in Miriam's life but also in many others round her. It is a sign of the times, that so many individuals are trying in various ways to escape and get free of restrictions and conventions. Many people with whom Dorothy herself was involved made a similar struggle, even someone as controlled as Jane Wells, whom Wells described as a girl 'breaking away from the tepid, shallow, sentimental Church of England Christianity in which she had been brought up'.

It is because of this restricted society that escape is a

dominant theme of novels of Victorian and even Edwardian times. The heroes of Dickens, George Eliot, Thackeray, Samuel Butler, Hardy, were most of them escaping or rebelling. In the works of the Edwardian realists—Wells, Bennett, Maugham—there was yet another set of heroes struggling to escape from mean or limiting circumstances, so that their novels often had a rambling structure, in which a constantly shifting background and the passage of time were vital elements, compensating partly for the flat observation that tended to mar these Edwardian novels. This flowing progression of episode, if not of perception, was what they had in common with *Pilgrimage*, whose author, when she first began to write her novel, was 'attempting to produce a feminine equivalent of the current masculine realism'.

The struggle against society's restrictions is movingly portrayed in *Pilgrimage* not only in the more articulate characters, but also in some of the humbler or simpler ones, such as Miriam's mother, whose whole life has been conformity, until in her last days she feels a sense of being trapped and of having 'been so useless'. Another such character whom we meet in the next section, is work-worn Mrs. B. at Tansley Street (Endsleigh Street), whom 'all these years of scraping and contrivance had not corrupted . . . she ought to be a judge', and who makes a similar struggle. In *Pilgrimage*, then, as in many other novels of that period, social themes are strongly felt, but the injustice, the maiming of people, is depicted in this work as emotional and spiritual as well as social.

In the last chapter of *Honeycomb*, describing the decline and death of Miriam's mother, Dorothy is clearly harking back to her own mother's death, in very similar circumstances. She had found it so painful to write, that initially she sent the manuscript to Duckworth as complete without this chapter, which she afterwards added.

At the seaside, where Miriam has taken her mother for a holiday, the people in their lodging house madden her, chattering their inanities, never waiting 'to know they were alive . . . But she knew mother was different. All of them knew it in some way. They spoke to her now and again with deference, their faces flickering with beauty. They knew she was beautiful. Sunny and sweet and good, sitting there in her faded dress, her face shining with exhaustion.'

But people's casual affection or sympathy is unsatisfactory. 'There was something crafty or worldly about them. They make a sort of prison. There was something true and real somewhere. Mother knew it. She had learned how useless even the good kind people were, and was alone, battling to get at something.'

Night after night, Miriam has to wake to minister to her mother and read to her from the Bible. By day her mother has mad conversations with herself. Miriam takes her to an old homeopathic doctor who tells Miriam that she must summon help, a trained attendant. On the way back to their lodgings: '... "it is too late," said Mrs. Henderson with clear quiet bitterness, "God has deserted me." They walked on, tiny figures in a world of huge grey-stone houses. "He will not let me sleep. He does not want me to sleep ... He does not care."'

Then comes the death of her mother; and Miriam is unable to eat or sleep or think. 'Moving her body with slow difficulty against the unsupporting air, she looked slowly about. It was so difficult to move. Everything was airy and transparent. Her heavy hot light impalpable body was the only solid thing in the world, weighing tons; and like a lifeless feather. There was a tray of plates of fish and fruit on the table. She looked at it, heaving with sickness and looking at it. I am hungry. Sitting down near it she tried to pull the tray. It would not move. I must eat the food. Go on eating food, until the end of my life. Plates of food like these plates of food ... I am in eternity ... where their worm dieth not and their fire is not quenched.'

On Dorothy's marriage to Alan Odle on 29 August 1917,
the difference in their ages scarcely seemed relevant, since
Alan had been given so short a time to live; and had it been
otherwise, she probably wouldn't have married him, she
was so unsure of their relationship, and not in love with him.

Their future was doubtful in view of his past life and
habits. He had never cared much for women. Charming and
courtly though his manners could be, he was essentially a
remote, detached person. Gravely ill and struggling to
continue his work, caught up in the Soho bohemian set
and drinking and starving himself to death, he had managed
somehow to keep hold of his sanity and his dignity, and
outwardly his equanimity. In fact he had been desperate in
1917 when the Army specialist sentenced him to death;
though typically he covered his feelings by making a joke
of 'his pay for one day in His Majesty's Forces—2s. 3d.';
and it was only his desperation that had moved Dorothy to
marry him.

The first thing to be done when they were married was to
get him away from London and his drinking cronies. His
friends still opposed her efforts to help him, calling her
'precise and pedantic', and it seemed as though she must
lose the battle.

But Alan 'now determined to drop all his former friends
and acquaintances', apart from Henry Savage, who was now
in the Army. However, as long as the Odles remained at
Queen's Terrace, it seemed impossible for Alan to break
away from that world. Dorothy longed to get away to
Cornwall, that 'region apart', as she called it, where a quiet
existence and fresh air might do him some good. But at
present they couldn't afford to go far from London and
their main source of income: the magazines that com-
missioned her articles and his drawings.

So they moved as a 'refuge' to the north London outer
suburb of Pinner, then still a village-like place, 'an old
place with character'. In this backwater their life, in furnished lodgings, fell into a peaceful enough routine. He cut
down his drinking; and they managed financially to scrape
through the week to Sunday evening when they always had
a bread-and-milk supper.

But there were stresses between them. She let her anxiety
show, about his health and the dangers of drink. What he
needed was for her to believe in him, and she couldn't yet
manage it. 'I, being by nature obtuse, and more or less
thoughtless,' she wrote later, 'tried . . . to discourage
opportunities for relapses and, probably, never lost an
opportunity of showing disapproval of drink.' At times they
seemed to do each other more harm than good.

Through her marriage she had taken on a new set of
burdens and chores. Alan's frail health and his impracticality
meant that she had to manage all their affairs, financial and
domestic. She, who had never been domesticated, now had
to learn how to cook, clean and sew. She was caught in a
worse trap than ever before, with all these domestic chores
added to a poverty increased by her marriage. Alan was still
'utterly unfitted to look after himself'. His earnings had
always been a pittance; and now 'the news of the marriage
leaked out' to his father, 'and the allowance was immediately
stopped'. She even found herself writing letters for him to his
family and friends, since it took him 'anything from a week
to a year' to finish a simple letter, and unless she 'acted as
liaison officer', he 'would altogether lose touch'. Only in his
work was he disciplined.

The Grads were also having difficulties in their marriage.
Veronica had flung herself into it totally at first, embracing
the Jewish religion and supporting her husband's ardent
Zionism, which took him from time to time on missions to
Palestine. But now the differences between them were
becoming more apparent. With their two children no longer
infants, they seemed to be heading for a separation. 'In the
end he grew very jealous of Dorothy and me', she would

Dorothy Richardson

write, as a partial explanation of the break-up of their marriage.

For feminist women it was not easy to adjust to marriage. Dorothy had not, like her friend, been an ardent suffragette, and she preferred men to women, but she had been much taken up with the problems and consciousness of woman; and she had written in *Honeycomb* that there was a certain 'tone of a woman's voice . . . nothing like it on earth . . . if you had once heard it . . . in your own voice, and the voice of another woman responding . . . everything was there.' Set against this was her 'longing to escape from the world of women', but at times it still seemed to her that women and men were so different that relationships between them were bound to be incomplete.

In these last years of the war, many people died of 'flu. Both Dorothy and Alan caught it again, and his frailty and her resolution to keep the marriage going were taxed even more by these illnesses.

A sense of uncertainty drove them back to their base at Queen's Terrace. They moved into Alan's old rooms on the first floor, the dilapidated grandeur of the former drawing-room, 'the prize room in a Regency house'. On its wide marble chimneypiece they assembled some important mementoes: postcards and snapshots, the bust of Voltaire, the Nefertiti figure. But still they weren't settled; and finally they moved on to Cornwall. To Dorothy it felt like a homecoming, back to the 'land of one's adoption'.

She was still writing *The Tunnel*, and trying in this fourth volume of *Pilgrimage* to portray the London she had first known in 1896, with all the atmosphere and detail that had made it so alive for her then. But since her marriage, she had had little time or strength left for her writing, after long days of hack work and the household chores that formerly had been a 'repellent mystery' to her. Her mind seemed less quick than it used to be: she noticed the difference. But Cornwall had always been her best place for writing; and perhaps at a distance from London she could find the perspective to evoke it more vividly— if only she could shake off her devastating tiredness;

and if only Alan could settle in Cornwall, though this seemed to her unlikely, as he was still tied to the London way of life.

But they had some idyllic outings, round Trevone where they were staying, as on May Day of 1918, 'when we first ferried across to Rock, wandered blissfully, quite lost, over the dunes and on and on, finally reaching Polzeath, getting ourselves back to Rock only to find we had missed the last ferry. There we stood, vainly shouting towards a quay empty of people, all of whom were making merry up in the town. What to do? Not enough money between us to put up at the little Rock hotel, not enough energy left to tramp the eight miles to Wadebridge to get home by train. At last, just as we were meditating a night in that large hollow on the dune, partly overhung by crumbling moss-grown sand, we saw, coming across the water, a small rowing-boat. Our eager yells produced a moving oar and soon there landed a wild-looking being, skeletal, with fierce red hair and gold ear-rings, who had seen us from the top of the cliff. A knight errant whom we had to compel to acceptance of our combined cash . . . '

Days like this gave them a sense of escape from all the old London pressures, and Alan too began to feel more settled in Cornwall. They had found a place of their own, Rose Cottage, 'a genuine labourer's cottage, one squat window in the front room, with a huge kitchener for warmth and cooking (and smoke!) and a cupboard in the same room for coal . . . No water nearer than the pump in the road outside the strip of long-grassed uncultivated garden. Outside sanitation.' She wrote of it eighteen years later that it 'must have been the gloomiest little hole imaginable; but this we never noticed and, each of us having for so long been an inhabitant of one room, we felt *palatial*.'

Alan was gradually finding a routine of his own, in daily walks on the cliffs, in his work, in the pattern of their evenings, the invariable draughts game at nine after supper at eight, and then talk. With immense resolution he had given up drink altogether; and Savage was moved to declare that 'Odle has more moral strength in his little

89

finger than most of us have in our whole composition'.

His health seemed, if anything, slightly improved. Dorothy was overjoyed, and shaken to find herself caring so greatly. In looking after him so devotedly, she had made of him a son as well as a husband. He could joke to his brother and sister-in-law about the child she might have had by Wells and the fact that Wells supposedly had settled £10,000 on each of his illegitimate children; but he was well aware that having no child made a gap in her life; and now he himself, oddly, was filling that gap.

Her capacity for wonder and enjoyment had always given her an affinity with children. She had used to take her young nephew Philip Batchelor on trips up to London which were memorable to the boy for the Underground journeys: they would always travel in the first, glass-fronted carriage, so that both of them could gape at the marvels of the tunnel with its dazzling strings of lights and its onrushing stations in the distance. With the Grads' son, David, she used to sing music-hall songs, wickedly teaching him one about 'Archie' to take off his stuffy Uncle Archibald.

She was at last beginning to receive full recognition for the achievement of *Pilgrimage*. In 1918 May Sinclair, herself a distinguished novelist, wrote in an article entitled 'The Novels of Dorothy Richardson', of 'moments tense with vibration, moments drawn out fine, almost to snapping-point . . . There is no drama, no situation, no set scene . . . It is just life going on and on. It is Miriam's stream of consciousness going on and on.' This was the first application of the phrase 'stream of consciousness' to a novel. The phrase had been invented by William James, writing in 1890 in *The Principles of Psychology* that 'Consciousness . . . does not appear to itself chopped up in bits . . . It is nothing jointed; it flows. A "river" or a "stream" are the metaphors by which it is most naturally described. In telling of it hereafter, let us call it the stream of thought, of consciousness, or of subjective life'.

The Times Literary Supplement, reviewing *The Tunnel* in February 1919, praised its author as 'one of the rare novelists who believe that the novel is so much alive that it continually grows . . . That Miss Richardson gets so far as to achieve a sense of reality far greater than that produced by the ordinary means is undoubted'. Later in 1919, the same periodical noted that *Interim*, the next volume, made the reader 'live from moment to moment, but every moment becomes exciting. In this intense realization of the moment lies Miriam's charm—and Miss Richardson's peculiar quality'.

Dorothy and Alan were living in a migratory way between London and Cornwall, keeping on the rooms in Queen's Terrace by letting them furnished through the winter and spring. He now shared her pleasure in London bus journeys. Sometimes late in the evening they would both be too tired even to talk or to sleep, 'and when I'd done my day's work, I was fit for nothing but a Bus ride. We went right down into the deserted city and over London Bridge, and saw a very nice young golden moon'. They would come back restored from these inexpensive journeys.

Dorothy had even, for a last time, got back her youthful looks. But both of them looked what they were : uncommon people : you would notice them anywhere, unfashionably dressed and Alan eccentrically shabby, his clothes usually looking, in spite of her efforts, as if he had slept in them, and his hair sometimes fastened back with a pin.

Just before the end of the war, the Odles were dining one evening at Fleming's, when they met the most rabidly antifeminine of Alan's old associates, T. W. H. Crosland, whose book *Lovely Woman*, an ironic title, had been a bestseller when it was first published in 1903. Crosland was a fascinating talker ; and he and Dorothy were deep in conversation when from the next table a young officer on leave, who had been watching her intently for some time, pushed across to them, brandishing a knife at Crosland and telling him drunkenly, but in an impeccable accent, that he didn't like his face. Protectively the man swayed towards Dorothy, offering to save her from her 'hulk' of a companion. She had the presence of mind to grasp the wrist of his hand holding the knife ; and getting up from her chair, she managed to steer him back to his table, while he kept murmuring : 'I'd do anything you tell me. *Anything.*'

A few minutes later he was back at their table, furiously jealous of her continued conversation with Crosland, and about to attack him again. The waiters threw him out by the back door ; he came in again ; and to Dorothy's distress the police were called and the young man was arrested. But it seemed that her old magnetism was working once again.

The end of the war brought a sense of release that swept away more of the old conventions. People were less easily shocked by works of art that, like Alan's, had formerly been written off as 'decadent'. That was an outmoded word of abuse.

In the very cold April of 1920, Dorothy and Alan came up by train from Cornwall to London. With his improved health, he had been working harder towards a first exhibition, and now it was about to take place at the Bruton Gallery near Bond Street. His work had acquired a new vigour and imaginativeness, and some of these drawings had an almost heraldic beauty. Wells, seeing them, was taken with their decorative quality, and bought two of the drawings in the 1920 exhibition.

Much depended on this first exhibition, and the moment seemed propitious. A number of new reputations were being made ; but on the other hand there was great competition and crowding for places in the galleries, with an upsurge of talent released by the end of the war. If the exhibition failed, it would afterwards be harder for Alan to emerge from the crowd.

Both he and Dorothy, coming up to London now, were cautiously hopeful. They invited some friends to make up a small party, meant to be a celebration, at Queen's Terrace. Meanwhile on arriving in London they found the rooms bitterly cold in this unseasonable weather. Their train fare from Cornwall had left them no money for fuel ; and at first they were dismayed. 'No coal in the house. Two small beatrice stoves hidden behind screens, with pans of water steaming upon them, created a warm atmosphere outdoing anything a fire could have accomplished, and making friends, with eyes upon the empty grate, gasp their astonishment at the summery warmth of the room.' Dorothy had learned these domestic shifts.

Their friends included some devoted admirers of Dorothy's, such as May Sinclair, whose use of the phrase 'stream of consciousness' to describe *Pilgrimage*, had in fact dismayed Dorothy, as she thought it a limiting tag, and later referred to 'that lamentably meaningless metaphor "The Shroud(!) of Consciousness"'. May Sinclair lived in a different world of affluence, with her elegant flat and her brand-new motor-car with which she was 'so thrilled', like the one that ironically Beatrice Beresford had predicted for Dorothy.

The party succeeded, but the exhibition failed. The two drawings bought by Wells were the only ones sold. The rest Alan never saw again : he never succeeded in getting them back from the gallery, its proprietor moving on swiftly elsewhere.

It was a setback, but Alan refused to be daunted. He kept working steadily, his health still improving. He and Dorothy had found something better than success. This unlikely pair, both of them natural solitaries, each somewhat bruised and disillusioned by previous experience, he a young man who had known next to nothing of women, she an older woman who had always found emotional ties with men unsatisfactory, he broken in health and she burdened so heavily that her own life's work was threatened—these two had grown to love each other deeply. They would sit together late into the night, just the two of them, forgetting time and place as they talked, like two young people newly met. After all her searching, she had found in this marriage 'a new world, the missing link between those already explored'.

At an exhibition one day they met an old acquaintance, Doris Cole, Alan's fellow art-student from Canterbury. 'Won't you congratulate me, Coley?' said Dorothy. 'Yes,' said Miss Cole, 'I think it's wonderful. Everyone talks about your books.' But Dorothy said quickly : 'Not my books. I meant my marriage!' That was more to her now.

Another friend wrote of visiting them at this time, and of 'the constant bubbling laughter of Alan ... every visit a little secret festival. It fulfilled a desperate need ... for charm and gaiety and intellect and a spiritual atmosphere away from the insanity of much of that time.'

The revolutionary anarchist Emma Goldman, who had been imprisoned on Blackwells Island in America, was now in England. Knowing of Dorothy's writings on behalf of women, she came to see her at Queen's Terrace, to urge her fervently to join the revolutionary cause, telling her that 'the salvation of the world rests with women, and can't come about until they leave off being solicitous over the welfare of their individual menfolk and use the energy thus released on behalf of *humanity*'. To Dorothy all this seemed empty and inhuman. She had come to believe that the most profound duty of women, and men, was in their personal lives. However, she agreed to see Emma Goldman again, privately, away from Queen's Terrace; but still she resisted her views, an ideal, it seemed to Dorothy, of a 'feminine dictatorship'.

The Odles' migratory pattern of living between London and Cornwall, 'each enhanced by the process', was working out well, despite occasional disasters, as in the year when they returned to Queen's Terrace in June to find their 'poor rooms and everything in them wrecked by neurotic lonely man tenant'. Another year, however, they were luckier, with tenants who didn't turn a hair when part of the bedroom ceiling collapsed on them, and who rented the rooms again the following year, only to be wakened one night 'when a bedpost went through the floor, suddenly'.

In the summer the Odles would pay a few visits—to Vincent and Rose, who were living in Buckinghamshire, to the Batchelors, or to friends in Kent or Essex. Dorothy, though always 'instinctively avoiding literary people', knew and liked the D. H. Lawrences, whom she had met probably through Beresford, in whose cottage Lawrence had stayed in Cornwall. She described Lawrence as 'an electric shadow in a room'; and of his work she wrote that 'Lawrence . . . is always himself. His style is himself and never a deliberately contrived effect . . . He does make his presentation of experience *current*, as is all experience if presented as a result of a sufficient intensity of concentration.'

94

She and Alan would travel down to Padstow, North Cornwall, in early October, taking a bungalow or cottage in or near Trevone through the out-of-season time ; and then in late winter when the tourists began to arrive and the rents were put up, they would move to a primitive shack on the dunes or the cliff-side. Here until the summer they would live in the utmost privation, often in unheated, freezingly cold rooms, with a mere lean-to kitchen with an open drain running through it. 'I won't say I don't enjoy the perpetual battle with *things* that is this primitive life,' she wrote to a friend. 'Only at times it seems too much and always it leaves too little time and strength for anything else.'

But they were free, and they were happy together ; and both of them were working, in spite of their setbacks, Within the space of six years, between 1919 and 1925, Dorothy completed and had published five volumes of *Pilgrimage*, beginning with *The Tunnel* and *Interim*, both published in 1919.

Her sales and earnings were so far modest, and in 1917 she had written to the literary agent Curtis Brown, who was at that time representing her, that she was 'appalled at the state of her finances' and could not imagine how she was 'going to pay her way next year'. In May 1919 she was still desperate for small amounts of cash and 'must find £10 before September'.

However, her fame had spread into America, although by an ironic chance, in view of the decorousness of her work, the serialization of *Interim* in *Little Review* from June 1919 to June 1920, had been interrupted when the edition of January 1920 was confiscated by the New York Post Offiec on grounds of obscenity. The target of this censorship was *Ulysses*, being serialized concurrently with *Interim*.

Her American publisher, Knopf, had brought out *Pointed Roofs* in 1916, and all the subsequent volumes to date. Both *Pointed Roofs* and *Backwater* had gone into two editions in America : better sales than in England, where, however, there had been second impressions of both *Interim* and *Deadlock*. Among other letters from American readers, she received one in 1923 from her old British Museum acquaintance Frances Gale, who had hesitated to write because 'the gentle, silent, self-effacing girl that in my recollection bore your name seemed to have nothing to do with this much discussed and quarrelled over luminosity . . .'

There was living in New York at this time an English writer a year older than Dorothy called John Cowper Powys, son of a West Country parson. In himself and even more in his younger brother Llewellyn, there was a Shelley-like quality of tortured imagination and fragile brilliance. Another brother Theodore, who had written many short stories, would soon make his name with an allegorical novel, *Mr. Weston's Good Wine* (published in 1927).

John Cowper Powys had so far written critical works, but he was now also planning a novel. He had been profoundly affected by the early volumes of *Pilgrimage*; and sometimes lecturing in some obscure American township on one of his tours, he would find that his simple audience were admirers of the work of Dorothy Richardson, who seemingly had the power to move ordinary people. Subsequently, when he knew her, he wrote to her on one occasion that he had 'found a very spirited little group in Minneapolis, Minnesota (a very Scandinavian place) who knew your works in and out and quoted passages in that particular way one likes best'.

Powys resolved to meet her. At a lecture in New York, given by the then famous John Drinkwater, he shyly approached Drinkwater with one request, which clearly annoyed the lecturer, who could not supply it : Dorothy Richardson's address. But Powys was determined to find her.

She was meeting more people nowadays, although her original shyness still remained beneath the sociable exterior that she had acquired so painfully. 'People, like books, I like to have lying about and maturing,' she said. To another admirer who asked if they might meet, she wrote that she always dreaded meeting people as she felt that she was bound to disappoint their expectations; so 'I should like to meet you, but am not so sure of liking you to meet me . . . Really dull I feel you would find me.'

None the less Sunday afternoons at Queen's Terrace became something of a salon, and young David Grad—'the child of Michael and Amabel* and, therefore, almost as much mine as theirs'—met there such unexpected celebrities as Chaplin, Paul Robeson and Anita Loos rather than more literary people, as Dorothy 'never frequented literary circles'.

One particular exception to this rule was Violet Hunt, a society beauty who had satirized some of her literary friends and her love affairs and lovers in a series of novels quite accomplished of their kind. She had latterly become the mistress of the novelist Ford Madox Ford, and she called herself his wife. He was not free to marry her; and she was dropped by Henry James for living openly with Ford, who had another, legal wife.

Not that Ford would have married her if he could. Violet was a natural victim, alternately vague and over-eager. She had some money and the lease of a handsome house, South Lodge, on Campden Hill in London, with Gaudier-Brzeska's statue of Ezra Pound in the garden; and for a time she retained the rather lugubrious, uncertain devotion of Ford, whose gifts as a novelist were marred by the heaviness and doggedness that also made him something of a bore.

He and Violet shared an admiration of Dorothy Richardson's work. Considering her to be 'the most abominably unread of modern novelists', he patted her comfortingly on the head when they met.

He passed much of his time in Paris where he and two of his younger friends, Hemingway and Fitzgerald, were the centre of a group of post-war rebels and writers representing a generation looking for new ideals to replace those which the war and its aftermath had destroyed. Most of them were finding these ideals on the political Left. Hemingway, standing in for Ford as editor of the *transatlantic review*, pressed Dorothy Richardson to write for him. He gave her carte blanche; he'd print anything of hers.

Dorothy and Alan had wished for some time to go abroad.

* Typically Dorothy Richardson refers here to the Grads by the names of the characters who correspond to them in *Pilgrimage*.

It was more than a decade since her last trip to Switzerland. The war had intervened, and the poverty of the years following her marriage; but by 1923 the increasing, if moderate, success of her books had enabled her to put aside some money for a trip abroad.

They were helped and encouraged in this by their friend, the novelist Winifred Ellerman, who wrote under the name of Bryher. She was another admirer who had diffidently written to ask if she could meet Dorothy, having heard the various legends that Dorothy 'spent all her days looking out of a window at a deserted street, that she never saw visitors or went out till midnight, that she was a man writing under a woman's name . . . but . . . I knew *Backwater* almost by heart, she fought for us [women].' Together with her then husband, Robert McAlmon, Bryher ran the magazine *Close Up*, and in 1927 Dorothy would begin contributing regular articles to it, mainly film reviews. The cinema fascinated her, not surprisingly, since her own writing was highly cinematic in its flow and immediacy.

Bryher and her husband welcomed the Odles to Paris in the autumn of 1923. They gave a big party for them at the Dingo, where trestle tables were put together to accommodate all the guests, the Hemingway, Gertrude Stein, Sylvia Beach set; and Dorothy and Alan were the lions: a dashing occasion for these two people whom fortune had always treated stingily. They had been so elated on arriving in Paris, the previous evening after midnight, that they sat on and on, 'blissfully alone in the Dôme until the small hours', two shabby quiet figures, taking in all the late-night life going on round them. This evening they were gay and expansive, the life of their party. Dorothy had even been shopping and bought a hat. Nina Hamnett took them about to 'odd places' they 'should not have seen without her help'; and Dorothy talked a good deal with Hemingway, still an unknown writer, realized how talented he was, and 'sternly pushed him on his way, protesting, and incredulous'.

From this pleasant triumph in Paris, they went on to Switzerland, staying first in Montreux and then at the beginning of December travelling on to Château d'Oex, where they rented Chalet Marie belonging to a local timber merchant, and found 'out here beyond the village a perfect stillness'. From the chalet, they moved on to a small pension, Les Hirondelles.

The atmosphere of Switzerland, as on that earlier visit when it saved her from a breakdown, did them both immense good. They were both working well here, and they aimed to make their money last till the summer, at least. There was news of a possible London show for Alan, a joint exhibition with three other artists.

One of these others was the Odles' friend John Austen; and word now came from Austen that there was a catch in the plan of this show, in that each of the exhibitors would have to pay some of his expenses. The Odles had not been prepared for this, and Dorothy wrote to Austen that 'the cost of living out here is higher than we had been led to expect. We hang on from hand to mouth. So it is necessary to confess at once that we could not face expenses "on the nail".' But 'I pine for that exhibition'. She was determined that Alan should have it.

He had embarked on a project intended to be his life work : a complete series of illustrations of Rabelais. His own style suited the work; and the first drawings were very effective, and frank. An exhibition of them might attract publicity, without which it was hard nowadays for an artist, or a writer, to have more than limited success.

By April when their friend Owen Wadsworth turned up in Château d'Oex, the Odles' money had nearly run out; and their dream of remaining abroad to work indefinitely was beginning to fade. Wadsworth was an up-and-coming journalist who owed his start to Dorothy, and 'as a lad on his uppers had slept on their floor at 32'. She had encouraged him to give up his job in a London shop and try journalism. Wadsworth, as a boy just up from the provinces and knowing no one in London, had been bowled over by his reading of *Pilgrimage*, and had finally summoned up the courage to write to Dorothy.

Invited to Queen's Terrace, he had been equally impressed by her presence—the splendid golden figure with

99

the magnificent voice and the expressive gestures. In middle age she had found her own particular style of dress and personality; and she was fond of wearing plain velvet dresses, most often brown or gold, that were cheap but effective. Wadsworth, at first overawed by her, soon found himself talking to her freely about his ambitions and his life. The minutiae of people's lives fascinated her: the everyday details that were all-important, in her view. But she in her turn gave little away to people like Wadsworth who took on themselves the position of disciples and to whom she talked of books and of music, the ballet, the cinema, *their* lives but never *hers*. She was conscious of the difference in age between Alan and herself, and still slightly nervous of his past, and so she encouraged young men like Wadsworth to call and 'be company for Alan'.

Turning up now in Château d'Oex in the spring of 1924, Wadsworth was amused and touched to see that the Odles had succeeded, as they always did anywhere they lived even for a few weeks, in turning their bare white Swiss room into a replica of the sitting-room at Queen's Terrace, with a similar array of postcards and mementoes set out and the same fug of Alan's tobacco.

To Wadsworth's astonishment, Dorothy confided in him that they were nearly broke and asked him to lend them a small sum to tide them over their return to England. He knew that he would be scrupulously paid back, but alas he had only his own fare and travelling expenses, so he couldn't help them out. It was a measure of her desperation that she should have appealed to him in this way.

After he had left, the crisis was solved when Dorothy received belated payment for an article. Alan and Dorothy came back to England in May, and Alan's exhibition took place in the following year. At last his work was attracting more attention—but not in very lucrative quarters. The small commissions he was offered, such as book illustrations, provided fees scarcely covering the cost of his materials. The twenties, expansive in most ways, saw a great rise in the cost of living; but Dorothy and Alan found their earnings barely constant.

The latest volumes of *Pilgrimage* had been well received. In 1921 in *The Spectator*, whose critic had been so dubious of the merits of *The Tunnel*, a review of *Deadlock* was headed 'Miss Richardson's New Novel', and stated that 'no one could read even one of her books and disregard her. For the thing which Miss Richardson creates in each of the books is as actual as the paper, ink and boards by whose medium it is conveyed to the reader . . . the perusal of the book amounts to a sort of vicarious living'. More impressively still, in 1923 the *Spectator* review of *Revolving Lights* was headed 'Proust, Joyce and Miss Richardson'. The reviewer deplored her 'tiresome twist towards feminism', but also noted her 'exquisite fairness and detachment'. 'When Miss Richardson first began to write,' he commented, 'her method seemed new to the greater part of her public . . . her technique . . . extraordinary in the extreme . . . Miss Richardson, passive and still, sinks through events and states of mind . . . and . . . reveals a layer of personality which is different to that either of Mr. James Joyce or M. Proust . . . What are the comparative merits of exhaustive M. Proust, modest Miss Richardson or stupendous Mr. Joyce? Each reader will probably decide emphatically upon this point according as he himself is most vividly conscious of one or the other layer of consciousness treated by these three writers. Each of us has a tract in his personality which corresponds to that treated by each of these authors ; but the point of emphasis varies.' In 1928 a subsequent volume, *Oberland*, was one of three works nominated in France for the Femina-Vie Heureuse prize, although no volume of *Pilgrimage* had as yet been translated into French.

Despite this recognition, *Pilgrimage* had not yet broken through to a wider public. There were periods when Dorothy felt completely drained by domestic work and by all the articles, reviews and translations she had to take on, to eke out their earnings. She resolved that these problems should not interfere with Alan's work, now that he seemed about to gain recognition. If anything must be abandoned, then let it be *Pilgrimage*. She was not only tired, but also a little apprehensive of the new world that seemed to have little

H

time for work like her own, careful and painstaking, and needing much revision. She believed that 'one must, as far as possible, come to what has been written more or less as a stranger from afar'; and she wrote in her manuscripts the letters 'I.R.' (Imperfectly Realized) opposite passages which seemed to her 'just summaries and catalogues'. But speed was the things nowadays, and readers looked for as much incident and sensation as possible crammed into novels, rather than a painstaking search of reality or character. The search, to be acceptable, had to be done in more abbreviated form, like the shorthand of Katherine Mansfield's stories, some of them expressing a lifetime in a few thousand words; or as in Virginia Woolf's novels with their brilliant elisions and compression: a view of the world that was more controlled, abbreviated, stylized by the author.

It seemed that perhaps the grand design towards which all these years Dorothy Richardson had been working, was impossible or futile. And yet she had to write to survive. Not writing made her physically ill. However, she was in most ways the stronger of the two of them, and the 'fear of failing my poor dear' troubled her more than anything else. If their fortunes were changing for the worse not the better, she would have to bear the brunt of it, and spare Alan even the knowledge of her weariness and shifts.

At this time, near the end of the twenties, the history of Miriam in *Pilgrimage* had passed these further stages : *The Tunnel* (published in 1919) opens with Miriam coming to live at Mrs. Bailey's lodging house, 7 Tansley Street in Bloomsbury, only a slight change of name from Dorothy's Mrs. Baker in Endsleigh Street. Miriam has a sense of inevitability and of reality about this move. 'You know in advance when you are really following your life. These things are familiar because reality is here.' At last she knows the joyful presence of London, though in her previous unsatisfactory lodgings she has been driven nearly mad with loneliness and thoughts of her mother, and also the blighting, disapproving quality of the landlady and other women in the house. 'I will never again be at the mercy of such women or at all in the places where they are. That means keeping free of all groups. In groups sooner or later one of them appears, dead and sightless and bringing blindness and death.'

Dorothy's first two London friends, Ellie Schleussner and her flat-mate, become Jan and Mag, living in Kennet Street (probably Kenton Street, in fact) 'across the square linking their street to her own'. Ellie Schleussner had translated some works by Strindberg ; and towards the end of *Pilgrimage*, re-affirming the connection between the real and the fictional character, Jan von Bohlen is translating Strindberg.

With Jan and Mag, Miriam has evenings of argument and discussion, again paralleling very closely Dorothy's own views and conflicts at this period of her life, as in Miriam's assertion that 'anything that the mind can conceive is realized, somehow, all possibilities must come about ... People who talk of empty space don't think ... space is more solid than a wall ... There's no such thing as eternal punishment.' Life is not a trick, and 'you cannot escape being happy and free. Fancy people being alive. You would think everyone would go mad with the joy of it.' But prayer, she feels, drives away that joy.

It is to Jan and Mag that Miriam talks eagerly of the letter she has just received from her schoolfriend Alma (Jane Wells) in response to a note from Miriam. Miriam, remembering details of their girlhood together—the references being to Dorothy's own school on Putney Hill and its liberal teaching—has some doubts of the friendship, remarking that Alma never really cared for her.

Miriam has started work at Wimpole Street in the surgery of the dentists Hancock (Badcock) and the Leyton Orlys (the Peyton Balys). There is the same easy atmosphere at Wimpole Street as Dorothy described in her own life in 'the friendly household of my employers'. But the work she finds hard and uncongenial : the exhausting rush to manage all the various duties, an endless wearying round. However, her relationship with Hancock begins to become more personal when he consults her about a Chinese plaque he has bought, and then he tells her he is put off by Lefcadio Hearn's sensuousness. Hancock is described as 'a connection of her family', and 'coming from the same Berkshire valley', all of which tallies with Badcock, whom Dorothy sometimes even referred to as 'Hancock' in her letters.

After her tiring work, she escapes into the London streets, the endless walking, the fascination of observing things, the cheap restaurants. 'No one who had never been alone in London was quite alive . . . I'm free—I've got free.'

When Hancock takes her to a science lecture at the Royal Institution (the British Association), she is impressed by the place and the people—and yet there is a limitation, even a deadness, about them. Her reactions to the claims of science —that 'science is always right' and 'to question that fundamental truth is irreligious'—reflect Dorothy's own view of science as 'dictatorial'.

But the lecture turns out to be about Daguerre and the '"development in the method of intercepting the light".' Daguerre, stopping the sunlight, breaking it up, making it paint faces in filmy black and white on a glass.' When the slides are shown, Miriam feels that there is 'something in this intense hard rich colour like something one sometimes *saw* when it wasn't there, a sudden brightening and brightening of all colours till you felt something must break if they grew any brighter—or in the dark, or in one's mind, suddenly, at any time, unearthly brilliance'. It's an illumination to her, and we see how much Dorothy Richardson must have been influenced by the development of photography, portraying light and colour and movement arrested in this remarkable new way.

But Hancock shows little interest in Miriam's enthusiastic discovery; and she is crushed by his admiration of a more artificially attractive woman in the lecture audience, and by his falling asleep in her company. She feels driven back into herself, wanting never to go out again with a man.

However, Hancock continues to invite her occasionally, his flat, like Badcock's, being in Hampstead. He is as diffident as she about their relationship, so that the affection growing up between them is an evasive, hesitant one. It shows us too how unsatisfactory she still finds close relationships with men. Hancock is another representative of the comfortable middle-class existence of her girlhood, and she is still sometimes drawn to that world.

Before long her own destructiveness spoils this relationship with Hancock. Another element in her also works against it : something ambiguous, masculine she finds in herself. When she goes to the theatre one evening in a party with Hancock and the Orlys, she is dazzled by the illusion, in spite of the excesses of the acting. So she goes again alone, having paid for her ticket by virtually starving for the whole of a weekend. The play is *The Merchant of Venice*, with Irving ; and what strikes her most is the reality of the feeling between Portia and Nerissa : so much stronger than that between the women and their lovers. She has a sense of her own identity as being something between a man and a woman. Later Dorothy wrote of her belief in the 'completely bi-sexual' nature of '"artists" of all kinds'.

Her first visit to her schoolfriend Alma and Alma's

husband, the writer Wilson, disorients her, making her view her own life with other, critical eyes. The Wilsons are very clearly the Wells; and he himself acknowledged this portrait as being one of 'astonishing accuracy'. Dorothy also confirmed the identity of the character towards the end of her life. The details of the house and the company, as she describes them, can be very closely identified with the Worcester Park and Sandgate houses of the Wells, and the set of people whom they used to entertain at that time, as described in his *Experiment in Autobiography*.

Neither of the Wilsons, it seems to Miriam, really cares for anyone, despite their bright protestations. Their guests too are putting on a performance, 'in their curious league for keeping going high-voiced clever sayings'. Yet she feels that these are her people : she belongs here. There is a fascination and charm about Wilson and everything he says, despite his opinionated wrongness and his central belief that men had created God. As the talk becomes more animated, an ardent young aspirant playwright seizes her hand, with tears in his eyes, and tells her she's 'an angel of dreams'.

The one ordinary woman, a young wife and mother, who comes late to the party, brings with her a sense of reality lacking in all the others; and 'Mr. Wilson knew that something . . . had it in him somewhere, but feared it and kept it out by trying to be bigger, by trying to be the biggest thing there was'. Finally Alma's over-intellectual, consciously superior piano playing makes Miriam long for even the vulgarities of Liszt 'whom somebody had called a charlatan, who wrote to make your blood leap and your feet dance . . . why not'.

Wilson admires her intellect and her experience of life, and urges her to write something and send it to him. But his reason for writing seems to her a wrong one : to create an effect.

In the Wimpole Street surgery she receives a visit from Mr. Grove, the strange intense young man who is based on the character of Fred Fenton, the best man at Jessie Richardson's wedding. Although he interests her, she feels herself impelled to affront him and drive him away. Perhaps his excessive sensitivity strikes too near home for her. She has her own morbid troubles at this time. Tormented by guilt and regret at her mother's death, she often happens unintentionally on the mean street with the 'Teetgen's Teas' shop that so painfully reminds her of her mother.

At an afternoon at Mr. Hancock's, she meets the art patron Miss Szigmondy, a woman of predatory charm—'something within her was moving so quickly that it made one breathless'—who takes her to visit a poor and ill but very talented artist in North London. They go on to the more prosperous artists' studios in Hampstead, and she notes the cattishness and social pretensions of the wives. In this world of painters, as in the Wilson world of writers, is the same social falseness and ambition that seem to her totally divorced from the creation of art, with its solitary depths.

She is saddened, at a Szigmondy party, to see Hancock impressed and attracted by a girl with a totally false charm and patter; the sort of girl who is dead to all real things, and who kills everything with her presence. There is a singer at the party, also known for her good works, who performs 'the worst kind of English singing, all volume and emphasis and pressure. Was there that in her goodness too? Was it a method—just a social method?' Miriam has a distrust of 'philanthropy', which reduces people and life to the pitiable. She realizes again that she must forego the easier, more charming Hancock and Szigmondy worlds for her own meaner but free life in Bloomsbury. These ventures into social life had made her less shy, but they have also disappointed her. From all these people, London is the refuge to which she turns. Through London and what it now means to her, she has begun to come to terms with her past. On the balcony at Tansley Street, during a peaceful solitary evening, she feels a new understanding of the events and people of her earlier years.

Still afraid of being tied, she now subtly demolishes her relationship with Hancock. When he invites her to dinner, to meet his relations, she greatly offends him and them by

being three-quarters of an hour late, through a misunderstanding. She is too stricken to be able to apologize. And so
she is estranged from him. A summer outing—a large
party—to his Thames-side Berkshire cottage only reinforces
her sense of being an outsider. And yet 'instead of an
employer there had been a sensitive isolated man; prosperous and strong outwardly, and as suffering and perplexed
in mind as anyone could be. He had not hesitated to seek
sympathy.' But now he suddenly changes the tone of their
relationship, with an unpardonable brusqueness. Suddenly
the surgery is a loathsome prison.

Miriam is adept at turning a situation so that the other
person seems to be rejecting her, and yet she has caused it to
happen in order to be free. This pattern will recur in her
life; and it shows her singlemindedness. Already she has an
air of purpose about her, that impresses many people who
meet her.

Impressive too is her immense if transient capacity for
happiness—in London and also on such occasions as a
seaside outing with Jan and Mag, when she wakes from a
sleep at the foot of a cliff, to find that the present moment,
in its intensity, can completely recapture the past for her:
above all, that first moment in the garden at Babington,
harking back to Dorothy's own early recollections of
Abingdon. 'Then *memory* was happiness'; and all the past is
made more beautiful in the re-creation of memory.

But at times she feels painfully isolated, set apart from
all her relations and acquaintances. In August, the dentists
having gone away on holiday, she has a moment of panic
alone in the surgery. This is set off by her reading in
Hancock's encyclopaedia the article on 'Woman', stating
that woman is biologically inferior 'mentally, morally,
intellectually and physically . . . her development arrested
in the interest of her special functions . . . Woman is
undeveloped man'.

Starting her holiday alone, she rides her bicycle to
Wiltshire, and has a feeling of happy escape. 'I am going to
lead a man's life, always getting away.' In Wiltshire lives
Eve, her second sister, the one who is most like their

mother. Eve, sensitive, elusive and touchy, has had a nervous breakdown. Though she is very much attached to her employers the Greens (who correspond to Alice Richardson's employers the Harrises at Calne), yet she is another who feels trapped in her situation, and she tries from time to time to make a change.

On one occasion, staying at a Decayed Gentlewomen's hostel, she becomes acquainted with a nurse, a pretty, ill-educated girl called Eleanor Dear, who indulges in fantasies about her admirers and her career, but also has a tough shrewdness that enables her to survive.

Through Eve, Miriam becomes friendly with Eleanor, another character drawn from life. In this silly, sickly woman, Miriam finds something to admire. Eleanor has, in a different way from Mrs. Corrie and her set, that creative power of women : she can make an atmosphere and a world of her own.

Mrs. Bailey is another ordinary woman whom Miriam, as she sheds her intellectual narrowness, is learning to admire. It seems the end of an epoch at Tansley Street when Mrs. Bailey decides to give notice to the lodgers—except Miriam—and take boarders instead. This will mean a new kind of social life opening out in the house.

At the start of *Interim* (published 1919) Miriam is spending Christmas at Banbury Park with the family of Grace Broom, her former pupil from Miss Perne's. But Christmases seem no longer what they were. 'Yule logs and then, no yule logs. Everyone, even the Brooms, were being pushed forward into a new cold world. There was no time to remember.' She finds it difficult to communicate her feelings and meanings even to close friends. Going out alone for a walk, she is saddened and alarmed by the North London crowds, 'their lives . . . a confident blind trampling'. Their certainty and their contempt for anyone who didn't live in their own circumscribed way.

She chooses to spend New Year's Eve alone and free in her Tansley Street room. But soon after that, in spite of herself and at the nadir of her lonely depression, she is drawn by Mrs. Bailey into the life of the boarding house, and offered breakfast and cheap dinner in return for giving the elder Bailey girl French lessons.

She becomes friendly with one of the boarders, a disreputable, volatile Jew, Mendizabal, who is amusing and original, and therefore interesting to her. Meanwhile Eve, once again breaking away from her sheltered life with the Greens, is about to come to London to work as a florist's assistant. Hancock understands immediately how much it will mean to Miriam to have her sister in London near her.

A lecture on Dante that she attends moves her with a sense of the supreme importance of divine and mortal love. Travelling back to Bloomsbury after the lecture, she has a sense of her own evil, her lack of love. And yet to become truly loving would mean 'being changed in a way one could not control or foresee . . . having things only in common with other people'. She has noted the obliviousness of good, loving people, their lack of real thought and awareness. And the limitedness of those who concern themselves only with humanity. '*Places* to them were nothing but people; there was something they missed out that could not be given up. Something goes if you lose yourself in humanity.' The Unitarians, the Evangelists are more interested in reform than in the wonder and the beauty; the Anglicans have more awareness, but 'are snobs and afraid of new ideas'. Perhaps, she thinks ruefully, the answer is silence for long years, through which might come understanding.

Back at Tansley Street, she meets Von Heber, an ambitious young Canadian doctor who, hearing her play the piano, conceives a romantic attachment to her. This Canadian and his colleagues, all staying at Mrs. Bailey's, refer back to Dorothy's own friendship with the Canadian doctors at Mrs. Baker's. Another result of her playing the piano is a visit to the musician Bowdoin's poor room in the Farringdon Road. Disappointingly she finds there a musical 'circle', another 'set' like the Wilsons' literary and political one, and like the artists of Hampstead. She is glad to escape back into her solitary London. But in spite of herself, at her first dinners shared with the Baileys and their boarders, she is learning to be more easily sociable with ordinary people.

Eve, arriving in London, disappoints her by evading her attempts at closeness. Alone in an A.B.C. cafe, she reads *Brand* and finds in it 'a background that is more real than people or thoughts. The life in the background is in the people ... There is something else; a sort of lively freshness all over even the saddest parts, preventing your feeling sorry for the people.' Background, then, like atmosphere, has great meaning for her: it is the fabric of the world that artists, and women, can create. But most 'men have no sense of atmosphere'.

The Canadian doctor, Von Heber, has created a background for their relationship by the somewhat unreal romantic notion that he has of her; and she enjoys this new rôle. But it is fitting that her misrepresented friendship with Mendizabal should ruin her chances with the Canadian, since she and Mendizabal 'are both *batteurs de pavé* ... both people who must be free to be nothing; saying to everything *"Je m'en fiche"*.'

She has a lively evening with the Canadian doctors, and she spiritedly defends against their criticism the London weather, all its weathers, including the beauty of fog. It is soon after this that Von Heber leaves for Canada without saying goodbye to her, because he believes mistakenly that she is having an affair with Mendizabal. Eleanor Dear comes to stay briefly at Tansley Street, and makes yet more trouble by borrowing money in the house. These incidents, of Von Heber's defection and Eleanor's shiftiness, have an ironic wryness that is recurrent in *Pilgrimage*, showing its author's view, again, of betrayal and inadequacy in relationships. All the same, Miriam is becoming more fully aware of other people, and more outgoing.

At the opening of *Deadlock* (published 1921) Mrs. Bailey has had a bad year, and the house is shabbier than ever. But she has found support in the young boarder Gunner, who wants to marry her. A young Russian Jew, Michael Shatov (a character based on Benjamin Grad, as

letters affirm), has come to stay in the house, and Mrs.
Bailey has arranged that Miriam should give him English
lessons. He introduces Miriam to a new field : 'philosophy'.

She feels that the life has gone out of the Wimpole Street
round for her. But her lessons with Michael take on a
magical quality of interest, for both of them. They read
Emerson, whom at this time she greatly admires. Meanwhile
daily events at Tansley Street bring her yet further out of
herself, when she forgets her reserve in order to tend Mrs.
Bailey, who has fallen ill, and she kisses her ; it is a moment
when we see Miriam coming alive out of her isolation ;
as if in readiness for the love affair with Michael that is
imminent. She realizes the goodness and the generosity of
Mrs. Bailey, whom previously she had undervalued.

Miriam takes Michael to the British Museum Reading
Room, that favourite haunt of hers, and together they read
Anna Karenina (Benjamin Grad had given Dorothy an in-
scribed copy of the novel). Being with Michael makes her
realize the incompleteness of her solitude. His differences
from her 'forced her to think. She reflected that solitude was
too easy. It was necessary, for certainties. Nothing could be
known except in solitude. But the struggle to communicate
certainties gave them new life ; even if the explanation were
only a small piece of the truth.'

Although less since Michael's arrival and her friendship
with Mrs. Bailey, the bleakness of her meaningless grind of
work at Wimpole Street has been spoiling even her pleasure
in her evenings of freedom in London and in her room. She
has had a 'recurring picture of a form, drifting, grey face
upwards, under a featureless grey sky, in shallows, "un-
reached by the human tide", and she had felt in her a
vain prayer that life should not pass her by.'

This Christmas she spends at the seaside town where Eve
(like Alice Richardson before her) is now running a genteel
shop, near the lodging house kept by Harriett and Gerald.
Harriett admits that her marriage is a failure, which they
only keep going because of their child Elspeth. But to
Miriam they seem illuminated by their life together and by
the presence of the child with them. Gerald has just bought

one of those new gadgets, a gramophone; and Miriam, hearing it for the first time, with its absurd strangulated singing of a popular song, is moved to laughter and tears.

Returning after Christmas to London, and as always overjoyed to be back, she is dismayed by the distraction of Michael waiting for her at the corner of Wimpole Street, and she tries to avoid him. She escapes from him on to a bus, so as not to miss the solitary moment of returning to London. Michael had wanted to talk. They have latterly been discussing Darwin, and philosophy and justice: Michael has a reverence for English individual liberty.

At home, she finds waiting for her a dandified Frenchman whose lecture on Spanish literature Mrs. Bailey asks her to correct. Michael has also urged her to translate some pieces. Spending an evening with him in an East End German-Jewish café, where she drinks lager for the first time and is slightly intoxicated by it, she talks brilliantly and freely, 'her voice alive . . . possessed and controlled by the first faint dawning apprehension of some universal password, from one bright tumultuously branching thing to another, with a gratitude that poured itself out within her in a rain of tears'. Through being in love, and communicating her own individual world to someone else, she has found a new meaning in it.

The work on the Frenchman's shoddy lecture is also a revelation for her, a new beginning in her life, as she makes something alive out of the dead, pompous phrases of the text. Working on it alone, after all the time spent with Michael, makes her solitary room seem once again to be the centre of her life. But she thinks that it would help her to relax more with people, to let go, 'not go through life clenched'.

In translating, in the actual writing it entails, she discovers a 'deeper convinced self who did, unknown to her, take sides on things, both sides, with equal emphasis impartially, but with a passion that leaves her in an entrancement of longing to discover the secret of its nature'.

She is dashed when Wilson damns the Andreyev story she has been translating as feeble and sentimental—but he praises the translation itself, and urges her to take up translation for a living. She is dubious : there is too much cheap hack translation, with which the public is perfectly content. Michael says : 'You are right . . . but you will not find cynical vulgarization of literature anywhere but in England and America. It is indeed remarkable to the foreigner the way in this country the profession of letters has become a speculation. Never before I came here did I meet this idea of writing for a living, in this naive widespread form. There is something very bad in it.' Anyway, she feels outside the world of writers, both the clever ones and the determined journeymen.

A basic difference shows between herself and Michael, when he says that she is perhaps too individualistic, re-marking that he himself believes in the race. 'Has the race not a soul and an individuality? Greater than that of its single parts?' His Zionism, his belief in the separateness of the Jews, is another barrier between them, though Dorothy herself, as we know, supported that cause. But Miriam is, like Dorothy, very much aware of her English-ness, and of how much it sets her apart from Michael.

They attend a lecture on philosophy, followed by a discussion, leading to Miriam's own conviction : 'If materialism could be supported empirically, there was something in it, something in matter that had not yet been found out. "Materialism isn't dead yet".' But matter, she feels, is inseparable from spirit. She doesn't believe in those separate compartments : in her view, there must be an underlying unity. Dorothy wrote, in a letter to a friend, of her belief that 'no beloved *stick* or *stone* or flower, let alone animal or person, can ever perish everlastingly.'

Her relationship with Hancock has become rather awkward. Rebelling against her employers' thoughtlessness, she is given notice to leave ; but she mollifies Hancock and is reinstated, though he is stiff about it. However, the dreariness of her working day makes her reflect that 'the power of London to obliterate personal affairs depended on unlimited freedom to be still . . . All the time people were helplessly doing things that made time move ; growing up, old people growing onwards, with death suddenly in sight, rushing here and there with words that had lost their meaning . . . Young men died in advance.'

Michael too, it seems, has his 'set of quoted opinions, beyond which he refused to move'. Because of their differences, he too is anxious about their future, and he wonders if she wants him to go away. But they are in love, and her love for him overrides her doubts.

Wandering through London, they tell each other about their childhood and past. At King's Cross station, before she boards the train for North London to spend a day with the Brooms, he tells her about other women, prostitutes, whom he has known. Distressed, she has to leave the Brooms after lunch to walk out into the park. 'She imagined herself raging and raving through the park, through the world, attacking the indifferent sky at last with some final out-breaking statement, something, somewhere within her she *must* say, or die.' Back in Bloomsbury, that evening, she takes pity on Michael, and forgives him. But this moment of reconciliation has an element foreshadowing the break-up of their love-affair. Miriam's attitude in this scene, and her forgiveness, are maternal. Michael kneels to her, humbling himself, which is what she doesn't want; but he has made this gesture, and their relationship is no longer one of equals. Now that she is dominant, she cares for him less.

So she quarrels with him about his limited views on women. She will not be talked round : 'I have nothing to say. It is not a thing that can be argued out. Those women's rights people are the worst of all. Because they think women have been "subject" in the past. Women never have been subject. Never can be.'

Once again she has undermined a close relationship, though Michael has offered for her sake even to renounce his Judaism. She cannot accept this sacrifice. But when— in the scene repeating Dorothy's own similar visit at the behest of Benjamin Grad—Miriam visits a Christian woman married to a Jew and leading, it transpires, a very circumscribed life, she sees finally that marriage to Michael is beyond her.

Revolving Lights (published 1923) sees Miriam beginning to glimpse some elusive pattern in her life : 'that without any effort of her own, so many very different kinds of people and thoughts should have come ... into the backwater of her life ... To what end was her life working by some sort of inner arrangement? It also seemed to be the mysterious friend, her star, the queer strange *luck* that dogged her path, always reviving happiness, bringing a sudden joy when there was nothing to account for it, plunging her into some new unexpected thing at the very moment of perfect helplessness. It was like a game ... something was having a game of hide and seek with her.'

She is attracted to upper-class mores and values, to that comparative largeness of outlook ; but on the other hand the complacency of that world is too limiting. She is aware of the conflicting heredities, paternal and maternal, that have formed her self-warring nature, and may yet in their conflict drive her to madness. On the one side is the Puritanism of the Hendersons : 'The Puritans were right with their vale of tears ... and more deeply attractive than the other side of the family. Their roots in life were deeper and harder and the light from the Heavenly City fell upon their foreheads *because* they struggled in the gloom.' It is clear enough that Dorothy is referring here to her own heredity, the Wesleyan Richardsons and the more superficial Taylors.

Wilson is now taking her advice on detail in his work. But talking to him about people saddens her, as it tends to reduce them to the level of the anecdotal. Formulating her earlier thoughts about the importance of atmosphere and background, she argues with him about women, whom she considers to be already emancipated 'through their pre-eminence in an art. The art of making atmospheres. It's as big an art as any other. It's like air within the air. It may be deadly. Cramping and awful, or simply destructive, so that no life is possible within it ... Artists, well, and *literary* people, say they have to get away from everything at intervals ... They can only rest, stop being artists, by getting *away*. That is why so many women get nervy and break down. The only way they can rest, is by being nothing to nobody, leaving off for a while giving out any atmosphere.'

Although she knows now that she will not marry Michael, affectingly he follows her everywhere, waiting outside when she visits friends in the evening. She now has an easier, stronger relationship with the Wilsons, and social life at Tansley Street is also busier again, with a return of many of the Canadians as well as some Norwegian boarders.

The engagement of Leyton Orly, the younger of Hancock's partners, is a pleasantly romantic affair, and gives her a glimpse into happy family life, reinforcing her belief in the traditional way of life as opposed to 'the new people without backgrounds'. But for herself, she still feels the limitation of relationships with men, who cannot share fully a woman's awareness of life.

Eleanor, her tuberculosis more advanced, returns to Tansley Street, where she entraps the Jew Rodkin, becoming pregnant by him ; and Michael goes night after night to sleep beside her. Eleanor, marrying Rodkin—as the original of Eleanor 'married Benjamin's friend'—moves into a villa at Southend, where she plays the part of an upright young matron. Eleanor, in Miriam's view, is more than a shady adventuress : she is a creator of life for herself and the people involved with her.

Miriam attends Lycurgan [Fabian] meetings, and the one she describes in 'Anselm's Inn' is very like the Fabian meetings in Clifford's Inn at the time when Wells was starting his attack on the Fabian establishment. Wells's own description of such a meeting, in his autobiography, is an interesting parallel.

Walking home from Anselm's Inn one evening, Miriam has a disturbing encounter with an old beggar woman, a leering ruined face that seems to recognize and reproduce her inner hidden self : her guilt at her personal failures, and also her disillusionment with the way the world is moving, as exemplified in the meeting that she has just left. Increasingly she regrets the destruction of traditional values. She is tending more and more to conservatism, so that her outing with Michael's revolutionary friends, the Lintoffs, becomes a kind of nightmare. She can respond to the husband's idealism, but not to the wife, who seems to her totally committed to utilitarian aims, allowing no place for the spirit. The day finishes in a squalid café, where the final touch, as she sits with a splitting headache, is the jabbering debased English of the louts at the table next to theirs. 'English is being destroyed,' she feels. 'There *is* a relationship between sound and things.'

Michael is to go away tomorrow; she has sent him out of her life. She thinks despairingly of 'Michael alone. With more than the usual man's helplessness. Getting involved. At the mercy of his inability to read people.' In the midst of these anxieties, there comes again involuntarily her apprehension of joy, of 'the extraordinary wealth of going on being alive'. But religion doesn't move her in this way. She recalls her inspiriting and yet finally unsatisfying visit with Michael to a Quaker meeting in St. Martin's Lane.

She goes now to stay with the Wilsons, and they all sleep out one night in the garden. Once again she feels a duality of repulsion and fascination with Wilson, and is dismayed to see him taken in by the contrived charm of the novelist Edna Prout. Miriam, writing a review for her publisher friend Taylor, is watched by Wilson who is amazed at her fluency. She tells him of the first review she wrote, for which she did a fortnight's research.

She and Wilson argue about this unconventional publisher Taylor (Charles Daniel) and his author Mrs. Boole. Miriam sees Mrs. Boole as a pioneer of modern psychology. She tells Wilson about visits to the Taylors and the wonderfully untrammelled atmosphere in their house. But when the Taylors' friends, weird cranks, arrive, then it becomes chaos, just as the Daniels' ménage had been. 'They all seem to be attacking things they don't understand. I gradually become an old-fashioned conservative.' She met them through Michael reading a notice of a meeting of London Tolstoyans. She admires Taylor, because he understands the needs of the individual, not humanity en masse. He makes socialism seem wide of the mark. Miriam and Wilson argue about socialism. He has begun to pay serious court to her, trying to encourage her 'womanliness'. But 'he spoiled everything by . . . his *deliberate* guilt and *deliberate* daring'.

Dissatisfied as she now is with her life, she wants to make it different. Any change is welcome, so she is delighted when Hancock, planning to leave his partners the Orlys and set up on his own, asks her to join him in the move. He is now married. But distracting her from these new plans, she has a note from Wilson, telling her that he's steered clear of a certain affair and that he wants to see her.

The Trap (published 1925) sees her moving into a gloomy flat in Flaxman's Court with Miss Holland, a prim but somewhat overbearing woman whom she has met at her club: the character based on Miss Moffatt with whom Dorothy lived in Woburn Buildings. The street name Flaxman she takes from Flaxman Terrace, a road leading on from Woburn Buildings deeper into the slums of St. Pancras. Miriam has recently been stirred and impressed by *The Ambassadors*, though also disappointed by James's complacency. 'But the cold ignorance of this man was unconscious. And therefore innocent. And it was he after all who had achieved the first completely satisfying way of writing a novel . . .'

She and Miss Holland pay a visit to their club, the Belmont (perhaps a reference to Portia and Nerissa, whose rapport Miriam had already noted when she saw *The Merchant of Venice*); the original of this club 'overlooking a Bloomsbury square' being Dorothy's Arachne Club, where she similarly entertained her relatives and friends, and where she met Veronica Grad, who was a resident member.

Home again at Flaxman's, and looking out into a stormy night, they see in a room across the alleyway 'the figure of a man appear from the darkness beyond the candle and stand pressed close to the window with arms upstretched and laid against the pane . . . He was dark and pale and tall and shouting at the storm . . . A brilliant flash lit up the white face and its frame of heavy hair. The dark eyes were looking straight across.' It is Yeats, and once again Dorothy is exactly describing an encounter in her own life.

Nothing of Miss Holland's seems to shine, to reflect light. The little shared sitting-room, to which Miriam had so much looked forward, is dead. She receives a visit from the Brooms, who are clearly appalled by the flat. But she takes them along to the club, which redeems all ; and she finds herself become something new—a hostess, which is 'also a sort of death, a shelving of the personal vision in the interests of social ease and smoothness'.

She is feeling trapped in her situation. Dr. Densley, urbane and attractive, warns her that she is over-working and heading for a breakdown. She often feels a dragging weariness. Densley urges her to marry, and invites himself to her dinner party at the club. In his own way he is courting her. He is Hancock's replacement, another in the series of conventional men who feel an attraction of opposites for her, as she does for them. They admire her intelligence and courage, and yet they deplore her unconventional beliefs and would like to see her shed them. Densley, who has in his consulting room 'idealized' pictures of simpering young ladies—the sort of the thing that Miriam hates as epitomizing men's belittling patronage of women—and who calls her 'dear girl'—seems to think that a happy marriage will soothe away all her rebelliousness. There are times when she almost would like to believe it herself. However, she refuses Densley's offer of marriage. (A number of Harley Street specialists were close friends of Dorothy's ; but if the character of Densley is based on one of these, his identity is not known.)

When he takes Miriam to a Lycurgan party and dance, she sees that they would fail each other in marriage ; she wouldn't fulfil well enough the rôle of rising young doctor's wife. She muses on what she is throwing away in Densley : the chance to rejoin the way of life to which she had been born. And 'free-lovers seem all in some indefinable way shoddy. Born shoddy. Men as well as women.'

At home she has to bear the bestial, violent night life of Flaxman's, the drunken brawling revellers outside her window, that drives her to sleep in the back room where the stench of cats comes in from the waste ground. But worse than that is the deathly presence of Miss Holland herself, who has been bitterly spiteful and moody ever since Michael failed to write a letter in Polish to oblige some American friends of hers. The details, of life with Miss Holland, and the surroundings of Flaxman's, very closely match those of Miss Moffatt in Woburn Buildings.

Finally Miriam finds the strength, in spite of her ill health, to break away. She will go 'away from this corner where she had been dying by inches'.

Oberland (published 1927) describes her trip to Switzerland while she is on leave from Wimpole Street: corresponding to the first of Dorothy's own two visits to Switzerland in the winter of 1907–8. Oberland is the Adelboden of her escape from the drudgery of her job, when at last she was able to begin her real work, writing. A later volume of *Pilgrimage* attributes to Miriam in Switzerland that same 'Sussex Auction' sketch which was Dorothy's first, and the circumstances of these early writings reproduce Dorothy's own. Harold Hodge, the *Saturday Review* editor who encouraged her work, becomes 'Godge' in *Pilgrimage*. Of her first morning in Switzerland: 'She awoke in light that seemed for a moment to be beyond the confines of earth. It was as if all her life she had travelled towards this radiance, and was now within it, clear of the past, at an ultimate destination.'

In 1929 Dorothy Richardson's greatest admirer, John Cowper Powys, who was still unknown to her, was planning after twenty-five years of exile in America to come back to England, though he would write to her later that 'there are aspects of the life of the people over here that . . . make me fierce to defend them even against . . . their own Anglophiles and Europe-snobs.'

He had lately joined forces with a young American woman, Phyllis Playter, who as a girl in her own Missouri town years before had found 'in a shop on Main Street' a volume of *Pilgrimage* and became an ardent admirer of it, long before meeting Powys; so that this admiration was something in common between them. Now, on their voyage to England, they were already planning with some trepidation to try to meet Dorothy Richardson.

The years in America had been hard ones for Powys. He had earned his living mainly by long, gruelling Extension lecture tours; and his writings, on literary and philosophic subjects, had poured out of him with a visionary but sometimes indiscriminate fervour. He had just completed his first novel, *Wolf Solent*, published in 1929.

He was a gentle, nervous man, who had originally gone to America after the failure of his marriage. His wife was an invalid and a Catholic convert who could not release him to marry again; and their son had also been converted to Catholicism and later became a priest. The companionship of Phyllis, a gentle but indomitable woman who was completely devoted to him, had made Powys feel that he might leave his refuge in America and face life at home again in England.

Dorothy, receiving his letter and reacting with typical evasiveness, 'basely invented an unfortunate absence from town'. But he wrote again, and he and Phyllis came to tea at Queen's Terrace.

He was not disappointed in the meeting. Like others before him, he found himself totally at ease with her. This shy, devious man who 'ran away from people to such a degree as to take the most fantastic measures to avoid contacts ... hurry down side streets, cross roads in mid-traffic, at the sight of anyone he knew', so difficult did he find human contacts, found himself talking as an intimate to her. 'Not handsome', he said of her : her looks were gone for good now ; but still he fell totally under her spell.

Even stranger than John Cowper Powys was his younger brother Llewellyn, who wrote travel books in a vein of moody paganism—*Glory of Life* and *Earth Memories* are typical titles. A few weeks later, Dorothy met Llewellyn at a party in Chelsea given by Hilda Aldington (the poet H. D.). On coming into the room, she recognized him as a Powys. The resemblance was unmistakable : the thatch of hair and craggy forehead and 'terrific eyebrows' and visionary expression. Rushing across to her, he eagerly thanked her for her kindness to John who so revered her work. 'Amazing that he should have visited you. He never goes *anywhere* ...'

John and Phyllis, after living in Dorset and then returning for a time to America, settled finally in a small council house in North Wales, where a few years later they were joined in the next-door house by Phyllis's aged mother and aunt from America ; so that ultimately Phyllis would find herself nursing three old people in this foreign land.

For Powys, Dorothy Richardson's work was, together with that of Joyce and perhaps Lawrence, the highest expression of the twentieth-century novel. But in 1930 Lawrence had 'done his dying, bless and bless him', Dorothy wrote. 'Only last week he was seeing, talking to, people—Aga Khans and H. G.s, and telling them he felt not ill but tired. So his end was very easy, I hope. Poor Frieda. She will feel dreadfully desolate. I am glad she has some children and some relations she visits, and likes, in Germany.' Dorothy had not held it against him that in an article published in 1923, in which he had linked her work with that of Joyce and Proust, he had found all three writers too

123

introspective, pronouncing grimly : 'You can hear the death-rattle [of the novel] in their throats.'

Powys became Dorothy's devoted friend as well as admirer. In the vicissitudes of his own life and career, he began to turn constantly to her for advice and for sympathy. They could not meet very often ; but the letters, passing frequently between them, expressed a moving affection. 'Deep my dear is the feeling and hero-worship that I have in my cold heart for you. It has been one of the great things in my life,' he wrote to her ; and she wrote : 'I am an extension of him, he is an extension of me, as you will'.

The succession of novels which he wrote in the following decade were some of them immensely long, extraordinary in their visual power and in their strange ideas. He was a colossus of a writer, and his books were works of inspiration, but flawed and uneven. Dorothy preferred his philosophical and critical works to his novels. She had to 'hide by quoting Alan', her own 'difficulty in getting through anything beyond *Wolf Solent*, bits of *Glastonbury*, and *The Pleasures of Literature*'. He was a very obtrusive novelist, given to rhetorical interpolations, and in some of the novels, which aspired to be epics of Celtic legend, there was more than a little grandiloquence, as well as many vivid and evocative passages.

His work had keen admirers and detractors, and his sales were uneven, so that he had a succession of publishers whose enthusiasms tended to wane after a strong start. He thought highly of Alan's work, and on occasion he tried arranging commissions for Alan to illustrate one or other of his books ; but these attempts would come to nothing. The publisher would change his mind or lose the drawings, and there would be another 'shock of hearing that Alan's almost-made contract . . . is off'.

In 1931 Powys published a monograph on Dorothy Richardson's work. He wrote to her from America, around this time : 'It's a mad situation : this of your works ; and one without parallel in *our* day . . . and what I can't get over, Dorothy, is the astounding calm way you take it . . . Blake, Wordsworth (in his early and middle life), Nietzsche,

Schopenhauer (I think)—probably you know the list of the Great Neglected better than I do!... Walt Whitman (only appreciated in all this land by Emerson at first) all of them damned and cursed, up hill and down dale, like angry troopers as the saying goes. But you just continue to go calmly on with your affairs as if you were that starlight on the ocean commented on by Matthew Arnold...' Again and again he deplored the neglect, to him incredible, of *Pilgrimage*.

She had written in an article published in 1925, that a woman's ambition is less than a man's, because of the domestic routine 'besieging her, wherever she is', whereas 'though a man may pass in a lifetime from the desire for personal excellence, the longing to be sure that either now or in the future he shall be recognized as excellent, to the reckless love of excellence for its own sake, leaving the credit to the devil—and so on to becoming, as it were behind his own back, one with his desire ... he is peculiarly apt to suffer in the absence of recognition'.

The neglect of her work was, as Powys saw, increasing. Her reputation, from its modest heights in the twenties, was now on the decline. The critic Louise Morgan, in an *Everyman* article of 1931, following an interview that Dorothy granted her reluctantly, could now write, of Joyce and Dorothy Richardson: 'There are two innovators in English prose of this century ... Whatever happens to the other writers of our day, these two will survive because they have not only done something entirely new with the English language, but have opened up entirely new areas of discovery to the human mind ... But there is one sharp difference between them. James Joyce is acclaimed on two continents, and Dorothy Richardson is, as she says without malice or regret but with a kind of matter-of-fact good humour, "entirely forgotten", though she is at the height of her powers ... It is strange that ... one of the few women of genius the world has produced, should come and go in London without the smallest comment. There are, of course, those who know her work intimately, and to these she is an incomparably seductive and fascinating writer. But the majority of readers hardly know her name, and have never met that colossal, terrifyingly alive, unforgettable character which she has added to the small group of the immortals in literature—Miriam Henderson ...'

There was less money coming in from the publishers. The latest sales of *Pilgrimage* were down, and she had to put aside the volume she had been working on, *Clear Horizon*. Of the previous one, *Dawn's Left Hand*, she wrote: 'I can now bear the sight of the volume, which filled me with sadness when it appeared and with miseries of apprehension beforehand, because it is such a wee starveling in comparison with what it should have been.' But she seemed more concerned for Alan's lack of success, as he made the rounds vainly from publisher to magazine to gallery, trying for any sort of commission from murals to menu cards.

'Even the advertisement line is now failing,' Dorothy wrote to a friend, 'as all but the wealthiest firms are using photographs ... Every opening is crowded with out-of-work artists and a job secured by one is snatched from goodness knows how many.'

When Alan did find a commission, it would often come to nothing, or else he was exploited, as by a certain gallery owner whose 'rate for the work Alan is now doing morning, noon and night is less than a living wage for the time required', and who subsequently departed for Australia taking with him all Alan's works in his possession, having said that he 'had a plan for them'. Dorothy published in 1930 a brief monograph, *John Austen and the Inseparables*, on the importance of book illustration, in which she mentioned the 1925 exhibition of works by Austen, Alan and two other illustrators.

Pilgrimage was still a long way from completion; but Dorothy was very nearly sixty, and had to spend much of her time 'haunting the museum in search of translatables for *The Argosy*' (of which at this time Vincent Odle was literary editor). In reply to a friend's invitation, she wrote: 'I mayn't be equal to moving beyond Oxford Street, where my British Museum work leaves me. This terrific heat makes the transit of London, for the very weary poor, an exhausting business ! At present I'm wilting, in a kind of despair of ever getting down to my own job.'

Over a period of four years, from 1930 to 1934, she took on a series of hack jobs, that had to be done at top speed, including five full-length translations of difficult works. One of them was a book on André Gide,* who seemed astonished that she took the trouble to query him on an interpretation. There were articles too to be written, and all this had to be fitted in with housework and with managing all their affairs : all accounts, all expenses, all practical planning : Alan still had no head for such things.

Despite the hard labour of translating under such pressure of time, she could still joke about it, writing to her friend Peggy Kirkaldy : 'Ask Bob whether he can't perform some kind of operation on the French language which would at least moderate the goings-on of the corps-de-ballet of prepositions, the "d'ailleurs", "ainsis" and "au contraires", posturing in soul-racking superfluity, up and down the page, indulging in every kind of elegant posture, including the coup de chapeau. Moi, j'aime le fromage, mon frère, au contraire, le déteste. To speak thus in English would be to invite reprisals.'

She would have liked to translate *Le Temps retrouvé*, the last volume of Proust's novel cycle, 'if only to turn that one volume into an equivalent of the style of Proust', now that Scott-Moncrieff, who had done all the earlier volumes, was dead. She wrote to Chatto & Windus ; but after some correspondence, the commission was given to Sydney Schiff under his *nom de plume* of Stephen Hudson. His translation was not generally held in high regard, and in 1970 the volume was re-translated.

Of Moncrieff's translation she wrote to a friend : 'Moncrieff was utterly honest and painstaking, and did good work in correcting the many misfortunes of the volumes whose proofs Proust never read. *But* he be-whiched the whole text, and "which" is the ugliest word in our language, also an incomparably stronger holder-up of the reader's consciousness than the relatively harmless "que" used far

* *André Gide : his life and his work* by L. Pierre-Quint (Cape, London, 1934).

too much by dear P., and can easily be replaced by the continuity-preserving present participle. Again, Moncrieff exactly describes himself in his rendering of the title "Albertine Disparue" (for Marcel a single, simple cry of agony) by "The Sweet Cheat Gone"! (one hears him giving a toast: "The *Ladies*, God bless them!")'.

Jane Wells had died in 1927, having given up that Bloomsbury room of her own the year before. Dorothy wrote that Jane's 'disappearance mattered dreadfully to me, and still matters, and will always. Though there was almost nothing we shared. Her life was a "work of art", and sheer poetry. And phrases. *Fabulous* shadows. I'll never forget. It is the uttermost about that sort of shadow in that-sort-of-environment—seen-as-secure. Whee.' Wells, now writing his autobiography, turned to Dorothy for help with it. She was struggling to finish a translation to a deadline, and she feared that if she wasn't on time the publisher might change his mind and withdraw the commission. But she couldn't let Wells down, so she put the translation aside to help him edit and correct his book. He had a commitment to go to Russia, and she was left, with the help of his secretary, to 'correct, comment upon and generally trim up' this immense work, and then correct page proofs and deal with all 'the business of seeing the two volumes through the Press'.

This done, there was barely time to finish her translation, but she managed it, and the last word was typed at 5:20 on the delivery day. Together she and Alan rushed down through the West End—an odd sight, this ageing woman and emaciated, shabby man racing along the Strand, glancing up anxiously at the clock of St. Mary-le-Strand. At 5:55 Alan dashed ahead of her, and burst into the publisher's office just in time to hand in the typescript before the doors were closed. They 'celebrated by going to the current Academy film'.

By 1934, approaching the end of her 'four years' hard', as in bleak jest she described it, she was ill with overwork, suffering severe headaches, 'dizzy and seasick with eye-strain'; 'and the five, men's books translated, and short

stories translated, and masculine Continental luminaries'
books commented on, have left me so rigidly set within the
"rational" approach to reality that it takes more than just
time to get back'. Moreover, a new anxiety preyed on her.
She was past sixty and Alan still only in his forties. He had
survived nearly sixteen years longer than the doctors had
given him; and it seemed a possibility that he might
outlive her; and what would become of him then?

His brother Sidney had died a few years before, living in
the house of a nurse who had cared for him devotedly. Her
devotion was so excessive, that when he died and his family
arrived, she screamed abuse at them, calling them ghouls
who hadn't troubled about him in his lifetime. Alan,
having come for the funeral, typically couldn't get his
suitcase to open in his hotel room; so he slept in his shirt and
turned up the next day at the service looking more crumpled
than ever.

It was yet another instance of how hopeless he was in
practical matters. If he were left without Dorothy, he might
go to pieces, not troubling to eat or look after himself.
The worry of it haunted her, and made her more ill; and
there were times when she felt that this 'hell . . . might be
more endurable minus mental lucidity'. But Alan must be
spared all anxiety. In writing to friends she adjured them to
secrecy over her illness—a heart condition and high blood-
pressure—and Alan must still not be told that she was
fifteen years older than himself.

She took on even more hack work, with the aim of
putting aside some savings for Alan. But someone must be
found to look after him, in the event of her death. There was
no obvious choice. His brother Vincent was also in delicate
health, and Rose had to struggle to raise her three children,
continuing to work as a teacher.

Dorothy's eldest sister Kate was nearing seventy, and had
to look after a husband of eighty; and their means were not
great. Through the years Dorothy had grown to feel
closer to Kate and to appreciate her sister's affection,
always 'tolerant and imaginatively sympathetic', that she
had so sorely tried when they were girls and Dorothy's

impatience of convention and social diplomacy had made her so difficult. Now she was more tolerant, even of much that she had formerly rejected as banal or second-hand. She had come a long way from the inexorable critic and rebel who had hated her family's way of making polite conversation to cover silences, as if these were shameful.

Perhaps this change in her was, slightly, a pity. Her hard life, in softening her edges, had blurred them a little. She herself noted that her intellect, her power to analyse and criticize, was not as sharp as formerly. Trying again to take up *Pilgrimage*, she felt that her mind had gone soft. Her writing, it seemed to her, now lacked creative abrasiveness, a temperamental edge. But she was more concerned for Alan and what might become of him.

She could not put the burden on Kate ; and Philip, Kate's son, the engineer, who was married and living in Ealing, was kindly disposed towards the Odles, but was not on Alan's wavelength. To Philip Batchelor, Alan seemed a theatrical figure, with his eloquent gestures and his shabby, bohemian, oddly youthful looks.

Veronica, divorced from Benjamin Grad, was running a hostel in Lambeth for street women, chiefly the older ones down on their luck, whom the police would often take along to her instead of pressing a charge. Mrs. G., as her clientèle called her, was a personage well known to the London prostitutes, who could turn up at her hostel for a meal or a rest, with no questions asked. Mrs. G.'s son was amused to find himself sharing this limelight. The Soho girls knew him by sight and would greet him politely, but none of them would ever accost him, out of delicacy towards his mother.

To a degree he had always felt as if he were more the son of the Odles than of his own parents. He had been a great deal with Dorothy and Alan, found them very understanding, and had a deep affection for them. He loved listening to their talk and discussions, in which neither would ever give way to the other, each preserving his own independent ideas. To David Grad, Dorothy's thinking seemed 'creative' and 'masculine', Alan's approach a more 'feminine', 'critical' one. But this was a distinction that Dorothy herself might have questioned.

Jessie and her husband were still in Texas. There remained only various friends who might possibly look after Alan, if Dorothy were to die, but none of them especially suitable. Probably the closest of these friends was Peggy Kirkaldy, the generous outgoing woman in whose cottage in Essex the Odles sometimes stayed. Peggy's devotion was such that years later, when Dorothy was dead and she herself was dying of cancer, in the terminal stages of her illness she found the strength to sit up night after night typing for posterity over two hundred letters that she had had from Dorothy.

Since Alan might therefore have to live on his own, Dorothy compiled a notebook of instructions for him covering various details he might have to cope with, and starting with such simple matters as how to write a cheque, and a breakdown of the pitifully small amounts of income he might expect to have.

In the mid-thirties, at this lowest ebb of their fortunes and of Dorothy's health and creative force, there erupted into their lives an extraordinary man, S. S. Koteliansky, 'Kot', who had been a friend of Tolstoy and was now a refugee in London. Living nearby in St. John's Wood, he had quickly established himself in the London literary world, taking a job as literary adviser to the publishing firm, The Cresset Press, an associate company of Dent's. He was exhilarating and exhausting with 'his dogmatic intellectualism and his big booming voice', and he 'leaves us feeling we have been passed several times through a powerful mangle'. To the amusement of Dorothy and Alan, he very soon became a mine of information on the publishing world, and at the end of a few months he knew 'the name and disposition and moral value and taste in hats of the second cousin of the junior partner's sister-in-law's half-sister by marriage, in all the firms in England and America, as well as their methods, bank balances and future prospects'.

He also conceived the plan that his own firm should publish a complete collected edition of *Pilgrimage*. 'In vain,' said Dorothy, 'I point out, specify, the number of publishers who have seriously considered such a scheme and have dropped it the moment they have glanced through my sales record.' Duckworth had been publishing her work at a loss, and it was agreed that Dorothy should take the next volume, *Clear Horizon*, to Dent. With the incentive of a possible collected edition, she forced herself on with the writing. The results were depressing at first; and 'Dent's, with whom it is due on July 1st, may find it too short and its last third too "thin", and may send it back to be enlarged'. Entire passages had had to be scrapped and rewritten; and other sections, she knew, were too cursory, but she had neither the time nor the strength to expand them. A deadline, such as Duckworth had never imposed on her, loomed before her inexorably.

The advance from Dent's was small, and she had continued to take on other outside assignments to eke out a living, but at least the hope of a collected edition was a positive encouragement. Then, after the publication of *Clear Horizon* in 1935, she learned that 'the "subscriptions" totalled 400, an amount scarcely perceptible by Dent's who, I imagine, will now feel disposed to postpone, indefinitely, the new edition. Meanwhile I hopefully attack the chaos of these volumes, resultant on Duckworth's efforts to standardize my punctuation, and my counter-efforts to recondition it.'

Her best writing time, she noted, was the autumn and winter, from September to March; and 'as one who suffers ... the tensions of mid-day, mid-week, mid-year, and is happier with afternoon and autumn, I like best the week's latter days, beginning with Thursday'.

She had begun the next volume, *Dimple Hill*, but it was going laboriously—'a different focus,' she told Powys, 'more aged, wider, less vital perhaps or, if vital at all, differently, I cannot tell. Anyway the writing of a somewhat ponderously moving stour old dame.' But again she had to put the novel aside for more immediate commissions, and she had to refuse another commitment when her friend Violet Hunt, long since discarded by Ford Madox Ford, and living on in her Campden Hill house in a twilight of 'wraith-like' vagueness (caused by syphilis contracted long ago in her Edwardian heyday) asked Dorothy to become her literary executor. She led Dorothy into a room filled with a vast muddle of manuscripts and papers, left over from her half-forgotten novels, and told her that there would be a legacy attached to the literary executorship. But Dorothy couldn't take it on.

In the autumn of 1937 the Odles, before leaving London for Cornwall, as usual let the Queen's Terrace rooms. This time their tenant was a young man, intelligent, charming, recommended by friends. After their return in the spring, they discovered that he had sold many of their books and Alan's drawings, including the best of the Rabelais ones and 'worst of all, *all* Alan's illustrated books, all of which were either privately printed or in limited editions, leaving him without a single example of his published work. It seems to be written that Alan shall be robbed.' The young man broke down, admitting some of the thefts; and the Odles, who were sorry for him, declined to prosecute.

Around this time, the Theodore Roosevelts, on a visit to Wells, had been much taken with the two drawings by Alan Odle that still hung in Wells's study. They asked to see other works by Odle, so Alan sent round to their hotel 'a selection of the milder Rabelais drawings, guaranteed not to burn holes in walls or endanger the stability of roofs'. These were then passed round at a dinner party, to the enjoyment and admiration of all the company. The Roosevelts bought four of the drawings, and asked to be allowed to take the whole set to New York to show at a gallery there. But on the eve of their sailing, they discovered too late that certain formalities must be completed for Customs. They were allowed to take only their own four drawings, and the chance of a show in New York was lost to Alan.

The death of Kate's husband in 1938 seemed the end of an epoch. Dorothy had long since come to terms with the troubles and *bêtes noires* of her childhood : 'those who knew one as a child . . . one learns to love as they deserved, even those of them one was graciously pleased to hate'. Batchelor's death recalled to her that time when her father was bankrupt and her mother's health was failing; and Batchelor, marrying Kate, had made over his own home to the Richardson parents.

'Knowing your love of cemeteries,' Dorothy wrote to Powys on 6 July 1938, 'I thought of you yesterday when, while London still shuddered beneath storm after storm, we buried at Thames Ditton, in a lovely old churchyard with sunlit ancient trees and this year's family of blossoms taking part, my eldest sister's husband. Aged eighty-two and very weary, having endured, with his always sunny fortitude, some two years of intermittent really dreadful suffering, he was glad to go. Not long before he died he saw, he said, waiting for him a daughter who died (by accidental drowning in her beloved river) in girlhood. It was a happy little interment, *enterrement*, how much more vivid is that word; nothing was there for tears . . .'

Kate's life had remained close to her roots—even geographically, the Batchelors having stayed in the west London suburbs. Through the years Dorothy, alone at first and later with Alan, had been able to revisit her youth by staying with the Batchelors, joining in their holidays and outings on the river, or playing piano duets with them, just as it had been in the world of her parents. Now all this was gone for a second time; and Kate, left not very well off, would have to sell her house; and there was 'a good deal of family gathering' to discuss plans for her.

Dorothy had recently signed a contract with Dent's for *Dimple Hill*, 'pledging us to deliver chapter etc. on July 1st. Begun three years ago and set aside for translations, it grew last autumn and stopped in December. Taking it up again in April, I have managed two or three hundred words on most days, but in regard to this last third my most friendly critics will ask what has happened to D.R. . . . What did happen was some kind of breakdown . . . To me the last third, dragged word by painful word, is dead.' However, she delivered the manuscript on time.

Dimple Hill is, despite unevennesses, a fascinating, oblique study in love and cruelty. Miriam, no longer young but still able, just, to pass as a girl of eligible age, is staying on a farm in Sussex owned by two Quaker brothers. The setting, we recognize from Dorothy's own life, to be Windmill Hill on the East Sussex downs seven miles from the sea.

Richard, the elder brother, marked by past disappointments but still handsome and a self-conscious charmer, is protected and spoiled by his mother and his sister Rachel Mary. The sister, devout and do-gooding, appears to be pleased at the prospect of his marriage to Miriam. It is Miriam who at first has doubts, urging Rachel Mary to send her away before it is too late; and then suddenly the sister turns, the family possessiveness shows, and their cold almost gloating disapproval of Miriam wrecks the affair; and yet the sister still apparently wants to keep her friendship in spite of preventing the marriage.

It is a strange and complex episode. Richard himself remains a somewhat shadowy figure. As for Miriam, despite her wisdom and perception, there is often an element of miscalculation in her dealings with people, because she is herself so different; she inhabits her own, larger world. In this episode she is seemingly the loser, and yet she emerges as enhanced and enlarged by it all.

In her actual life, in the face of disappointments and hardships, Dorothy Richardson had managed to create the sort of world she believed in—a generous, large-minded atmosphere, a richness of detail, a marriage of noble devotion on both sides—although the materials from which she had created that life were very scant. Alan was a ghost of a man, and in spite of his talent he had failed in his career. Her great novel was far from completion. She was old and her work was half-forgotten. She continually re-affirmed the wonder and the beauty of the world; but her poverty and hack work and all the domestic shifts and drudgery had kept her from enjoying it freely. She had so deep a religious sense that she belonged to all religions and to none. Her dearest, most intimate friend now considered and would subsequently write, in bitter retrospect, that Dorothy had ruined her life. She admired the ordinary and the simple in human behaviour; but she herself instinctively held back from close human contact. People would confide in her; but she would rarely give anyone her confidence, believing as she did that one's inmost self is lost and not found in close relationships. She thought much of honesty and courage, and practised these qualities, but she had many times escaped and evaded situations. Her manner was magnificent, but she was a gracious lady living in broken-down shacks and a crumbling London hovel. Thinking, she wrote, is an enemy of living; but that enemy had mastered too much of her own life. It was a glorious façade she had built, transforming her losses and her lacks into splendours, just as she had made herself, by willing it, physically more splendid and impressive and golden in her middle years than she had been in her youth. She was a marvellous creator, and like all of that species she lived very much among wilful illusions.

But she knew how many-faceted was truth, about everything, even herself.

Miriam too had been creating a different sort of life for herself in the volumes of *Pilgrimage* published through the thirties. *Dawn's Left Hand* (published 1931) sees her returning to England from Switzerland resolved on this change, and finding London and everyone about her transformed by her re-kindled vision. Back in her room in Flaxman's, which she now loathes, she finds waiting for her a love letter from Wilson. But she wants to put him off for the time being.

Going to see Densley, she learns that Eleanor has died of tuberculosis, as did the original of Eleanor. When Densley proposes to her a second time, she is very near to accepting and being safe at last, but again she refuses him. Afterwards, on her way back to the Wimpole Street surgery, she finds herself in the Teetgen's Teas alley, the place that had always reminded her of her mother's death; but its power is now exorcised, the power that had 'forced me to gaze into the darkest moment of my life and to remember that I had forfeited my share in humanity for ever and must go quietly and alone until the end . . . And now their power has gone. They can bring back only the memory of a darkness and horror, to which, then, something has happened, begun to happen.'

The Wilsons, courting her, take her out to dinner at a smart restaurant, and then on to a box at Covent Garden, to hear Wagner.

But now there appears upon the scene someone far more attractive and interesting to Miriam than Wilson ever was. This girl Amabel, recently come back to London after studying in Paris, is living at Miriam's club. Her background and romantic involvements, her suffragette fervour leading up to her arrest and imprisonment, her period of skivvying for Mrs. B. at Tansley Street: all this is very reminiscent of

Veronica Grad. Miriam even calls Amabel by the same pet name 'Babinka' that Dorothy used for Veronica. And when Miriam has at last escaped from Flaxman's and the squalid shared flat, she and Amabel live together at Tansley Street.

And yet Amabel's almost instant adoration of her has saddened her a little. For rather than be 'committed for life to the rôle allotted to her' by this girl, she would prefer to escape 'back into the company of people who moved mostly along the surface levels and left her to herself'.

On the day of her leaving Flaxman's, she reflects on how little impression its sounds, among other aspects, have made on her. She can even now recall distinctly the varying sounds of the different Tansley Street doors . . . Going into her room, she sees that Amabel, who had called in her absence, has scrawled on the looking-glass a love letter to her.

Wilson takes her to dinner in the private room of a restaurant. She reflects on how much her life has been interwoven through his own crucial past ten years, the period of his rise from obscurity to success. And yet he doesn't really know her. 'For so dismally, in everyone, he saw only what they were becoming or might become, and of the essential individual knew, and wanted to know, nothing at all.'

But now for once he tries to join her in silence. She keeps thinking of Amabel and 'her certainty that between men and women there can be no direct communication'. She pities Wilson in his isolation, and remembers that he has written her a letter, arranging this evening, which shows that he has a deeper self too, though he forswears it. At this moment she hears a street musician play a little aria, a piece that her dead sister Eve used to play ; and it shows her, by the force of her reaction, how much stronger and deeper is the past than these 'raw new years'. Wilson is delighted by her absorption in the tune, and says he envies her power of enthusiasm at a moment's notice.

When they embrace, naked, she is touched by a sense of his helplessness ; and once again, as with Michael, her affection for him has an almost maternal note. They go on, unconsummated, to Donizetti's, one of her own, poorer haunts ; and he talks to her of her writing a novel, but she sees it as a 'dreadful enclosure'. 'The torment of *all* novels is what is left out . . . Bang, bang, bang, on they go, these men's books, like an L.C.C. tram, yet unable to make you forget them, the authors, for a moment.' She tells Wilson that she's preoccupied with Amabel. She recalls moments of extraordinary closeness to Amabel. None the less it is the affair with Wilson, and the awakening it brings her, that makes her begin to move away from Amabel.

On a night when she is staying with the Wilsons, he comes into her room and makes love to her. She wakes in the morning to find the scene bleak and empty. All day he deliberately keeps away from her: 'to demonstrate a principle: elimination of the personal.'

But she forgets her anger and her sense of loss in a tram journey along the coast, watching the light and the scene. Back in London, she feels enhanced, and able to escape from her anxieties, to range 'through her London, her beloved territory, without let or hindrance'. She has not yet found the relationship she is seeking—corresponding to the unity of matter and spirit in which she believes—that will reconcile the opposites of two separate beings, and of woman and man.

Near the opening of *Clear Horizon* (published 1935), she discovers that she is pregnant, and she feels joyfully impelled to write to Michael telling him her news. Over the years Michael has sent her a series of telegrams heralding each new trouble or problem or disaster in his life, and each time summoning her for help. But now, writing to him without mentioning her pregnancy, it comes to her that she will introduce him to Amabel.

Though at their first meeting they don't seem to make any contact, Amabel amazes Miriam by telling her that she, Miriam, must marry him. Despite Miriam's refusal to acknowledge this statement, Amabel pronounces that he's wonderful and beautiful. Filled suddenly with an incredulous hope, Miriam says: 'Then marry him, my dear, yourself.'

Miriam goes on with Michael to a concert, and it is spoiled for her by that same deadness that came over her on the morning after she first slept with Wilson. She will have to find the courage 'not so much to steel herself against the withdrawal of the old familiar magnetic stream as to push on, in spite of its withdrawal, to the discovery of some new way of being'. Her awareness of the music is disappointingly shallow—until a little phrase of unaccompanied flute strikes through to her, and helps her back towards the profound solitude, in which after all she now sees she must bear her child.

In the interval of the concert, she tells Michael her news, and he is deeply moved. He asks her to marry him 'as brother. At once'. Leaving the concert, they walk into Regent's Park, and the light, and the scene of spring, restore everything to her 'with a more smiting intensity than when she had first come upon them'.

Miriam's pregnancy comes to an end—presumably by a miscarriage, though no details are given—shortly before the evening when she introduces Amabel to Wilson for the first time, and Amabel lets her down by over-reacting and talking too wildly. Wilson, deeply disappointed when he learns that Miriam's pregnancy is at an end, takes her on to Donizetti's, where, avoiding personal conversation, she tells him about her Somerset grandmother who was 'no older at the end of life' than she was as a child. She says, as a comment on the separate worlds that people like Wilson and herself inhabit: 'It's finding the *same* world in another person that moves you to your roots.'

She and Wilson have never had such an affinity. Emerging from the restaurant, she longs to get away from him back into her own London, despite his offers to see her home. She braces 'herself against the truth of their relationship, the essential separation and mutual dislike of their two ways of being, remembering how in earlier days he had mysteriously insisted that a relationship can be "built up"'.

Amabel proudly carries a banner in the Suffragette procession; with Miriam, this once, marching behind her; and many ordinary pedestrians, including men, are moved to join the ranks. Soon afterwards, Amabel is arrested for demonstrating, and sentenced to a fortnight in Holloway

Prison. Miriam, visiting her there, finds her irrepressibly posing as a martyr; though the conditions are heart-breaking. But suddenly the woodenness of their interview is too much for them, and they both burst out laughing.

Wilson has sent her a note stating that 'the real difference between us is that while you think in order to live, I live in order to think'. She, she reflects, would 'see his world of ceaseless "becoming" exchanged for one wherein should be included also the fact of "being"'. Sending back his post-card, she proposes to destroy his other letters. (Dorothy's own comment on this incident, a few years after writing *Clear Horizon*, was that 'M., vain, ill-tempered, brotherless little idiot, sent back Hypo's note on account of its *tone*!')

So his world is now closed to her, as is Hancock's since his marriage, 'and the one she had inhabited with Amabel was breaking up'. Amabel, it seems, has also deliberately broken the casket that held Wilson's letters, in order to read them. Miriam bitterly regrets the old casket that had been her grandmother's. 'Perhaps in the end, things, like beloved backgrounds, are people. But individual objects hold the power of moving one deeply and immediately and always in the same way. There is no variableness with them, neither shadow of turning. People move on variously and intermittently and, in direct confrontation, there is nearly always a barrier. In things, even in perfectly "ordinary and commonplace" things, life is embodied.' She expresses here the animism that was one of Dorothy's own central beliefs.

When Miriam goes to see Densley, who has been treating her sister Sarah, he comments with shock on Miriam's seriously run-down condition. He prescribes rest: six months at least. His prescription of a rest, she sees, can be her escape and rescue. She has some insurance money that she has painfully saved over the years.

Thus after ten years—she reflects back over them—she is leaving Wimpole Street at last. Wilson had kindly offered to lend Hancock his own secretary for six months. She pays a farewell visit to the Wilsons, and it is a moment of pleasant, relaxed rapprochement.

Her goodbye to Hancock is more deeply felt. 'Although

this was the end, his good wishes, still more to her than those of anyone in the world, would somehow follow and bless her wayfaring.'

The *Dimple Hill* volume (published in 1938) opens with a weekend spent at the Brooms' house at Banbury Park, and then a week with them in and around a south coast Cathedral city. On her own again, Miriam goes to stay at Dimple Hill on the Sussex Downs. She is much occupied at present with the problems of writing. Reflecting on novels and novelists, she finds even Tolstoy 'enclosed, as all great novelists seem to be, in a world of people. People related only to each other. Human drama, in a resounding box. Or under a silent sky.' But Dostoievsky is more satisfying in that he 'does not judge his characters. Whatever, wherever they are, one feels light somehow present in and about them ; irradiating.' She herself, seeing a patch of light at the top of some distant trees, is oddly moved by this view—it seems almost a vision of God.

Of another writer she remarks that by 'expressing nature in terms of fantasy, he robs it ... The horns of elfland faintly blowing, in the mind that yet believes the sound of a tin whistle to be the more moving.' Miriam, about to embark on her own writing, expresses Dorothy's view of imagination : that fanciful, unreal elements are no part of it. A belief in life itself, 'the ultimate astonisher', has come to be Miriam's creed ; as Dorothy wrote elsewhere that 'the meaning of a belief is a life'.

Of all religious sects, Miriam has felt most affinity to the Friends ; and she is drawn to them again as she becomes a boarder at the Dimple Hill (Windmill Hill) farm of the Quaker family, the Roscorlas, drawn from Dorothy's friends, the Penroses. The details of the place and the family are, again, so similar, that this chapter provides a commentary, or counterpoint, to that episode of Dorothy's life.

This peaceful, country background enables Miriam to relax as never before. She muses on 'whether, when socialism came and everyone was a worker, there would be any joy left uncontaminated?' As to her feminism, she now discovers that 'I no longer care ... Could this be true? Summoning the hitherto infallible inspirers of wrath, things read incredulously, opinions, roundly expressed or casually implied, she found that they failed to move her. Deprived of their old power, lustreless, deflated, they seemed now only the harsh and pitiful echoes of a world from which for ever she had escaped.'

As she becomes more a part of the Roscorla household, she even asks the sister Rachel Mary for a pail and scrubbing brush, to scrub out the summer house.

The news of the engagement of Amabel and Michael has overjoyed her and also disturbed her with jealousy, even though she had brought it about. She recalls how quite recently Michael had said to her: 'Miriam, even now is it too late? To sit with you for an hour, to hold your hand and see your eyes, is more to me than a lifetime with this charming girl.'

Michael comes for a weekend to Dimple Hill; and 'looking from her window, early on Sunday morning before anyone was about, Rachel Mary had seen "Mr. Shatov" out on the lawn alone, believing himself unobserved ... *dancing*. A lonely little Jew, jigging about on her lawn, solemnly, clumsily, and yet with an appealing grace, the heavy bulk of his body redeemed by the noble head, face uplifted to the sky, beard-point extended in the alien Sussex air; rejoicing before the Lord, with the Tablets of the Law invisibly held within his swaying arms.'

Amabel's visit—again corresponding to a visit by Veronica to the Penrose farm—is less satisfactory. She comments on the Roscorlas: 'No, Mira ... There's only one thing I couldn't stand. My God, those *awful* silences!'

Having scrubbed out the summer house, Miriam begins to write in it, but 'this mass of hurriedly written pages' still seems to her false, 'skating along surfaces to a superstitious finality'. If she were to follow up these pages, 'everything would be left out that is always there, preceding and accompanying and surviving the drama of human relationships; the reality from which people move away as soon as they closely approach and expect each other to be all in all.'

She hears now about Rachel Mary's missionary years in London ; and Rachel Mary says to her gently : 'I've never had a musical sister-in-law, I have always wanted one.' But Miriam's remark that 'Money ought not to be saved', misunderstood by the Roscorlas, shocks and alienates them all, and Richard goes away abruptly to stay with a married brother in suburban London. However, the misunderstanding passes ; he returns, and they all have a glorious picnic. Now it is Miriam's turn to try to resist becoming involved with him.

She spends some days in London with Michael and Amabel, and they go on the first evening to Donizetti's, both of them fêting her. But Amabel, briefly alone with her, shows an ugly haste to assure her that Michael now shares her views and no longer Miriam's. 'You know, Mira, we find Emerson *trite*.' As if to say : 'So much for your Emerson, and Michael, who used so enormously to admire him, agrees with *me*. In place of your Michael, who has ceased to exist, another has come into being.'

But later when they are alone together in the old Flaxman room for the night, there is a sense of complete union between herself and Amabel : 'Completeness of being . . . with the whole universe between us, within us, in a way woman and man, be they never so well mated, can never have. In a few hours Amabel will be isolated, for life, with an alien consciousness.' Veronica described these relationships in similar terms, writing many years later but with her feelings still undimmed.

This evening, when Miriam thinks of Richard, he is by comparison reduced to nothing, apart from his surroundings, his background, which mean more to her than himself.

On the next morning, Amabel's wedding day, Amabel and Miriam go together to the public baths in the Euston Road, and Amabel sings in her cubicle.

After the wedding, Miriam spends her spare hour before the train at a Lycurgan meeting, and is totally alienated by it. A note is passed to her by Wilson, whom she had not seen among the audience. He too is sending in his resignation from the Lycurgans; just as, in 1908, the year of Veronica's marriage to Benjamin Grad, Wells resigned from the Fabian Society.

Miriam returns to Dimple Hill, to the situation of gradual change and betrayal on the part of the Roscorlas, as already described.

There were hopes of a success for the collected edition of *Pilgrimage*, published in four volumes in 1938. Dent had prepared a publicity brochure for booksellers and the Press. There were included impressive quotations from Hugh Walpole and Virginia Woolf; from Wells: 'They ... mark an epoch in the technical development of the novelist's art, a real and successful thrust toward a new reality and intensity of rendering that has exerted a powerful influence upon a multitude of contemporary writers'; from Rebecca West: 'This work has established itself as one of the real achievements of the time ... a miracle of performance'; and from Frank Swinnerton: 'Miss Dorothy Richardson's work is like nothing else in modern literature. It has a precision, and a brilliant, inexorable veracity, to which no other writer attains. It is bound to influence novelists of the future (as it has influenced those of the present) ... Of its importance there is no question.'

Receiving the brochure, Dorothy was taken aback to see it stated that the work was complete. Dent mistakenly had thought this was so, and they now prevailed upon her to agree that the wording should stand. It would help to sell the edition, which was published in the autumn, Knopf having taken sheets to publish in America. Sales began slowly. However, in December *The Times Literary Supplement* devoted a leading article to *Pilgrimage*, describing it as a 'prodigious and austere' achievement.

Meanwhile, the Odles had suffered a blow. The Estate who owned Queen's Terrace had done no further redevelopment in the road since the building of the War Office block twenty-one years before. Now, faced with steeply rising costs of maintaining the old houses, they planned to demolish the rest of that part of the terrace which included 32. If this happened, the Odles would lose their one permanent home. Their deepest roots were here in Queen's Terrace where Dorothy had lived for twenty-five years and Alan for thirty. Without a base in London—and everything they heard of was far too expensive for them—they would simply be migrants between shacks and cottages in Cornwall.

They stood out as long as they could against eviction. The executors of the Estate were obliged to keep them on when everyone else had moved out, including their neighbours downstairs, 'taking with them our friend the thief' of Alan's drawings. He had gone to the ground-floor tenants as a lodger when typically the Odles had refused to take action against him. Alan was only now discovering the full extent of the theft, and it moved him to say—very strong words for him : 'That *does* make me feel like *hating* him.'

All the lower windows of the house were boarded up, and the surrounding houses were deserted. The silence was unnerving at night, in the derelict road with all its peeling and broken façades. There were thieves about, breaking into houses in this desolate area. But Dorothy and Alan resolutely stayed on—to the annoyance of the Estate, who complained at the cost of the water rate; until in the autumn of 1938, they went down to Cornwall. That annual migration was too much a part of their lives to be changed.

In their absence David Grad was left in charge of their rooms. He reported to them that the road was to be renamed Forsyte, in honour of Galsworthy. Actually, the new name was Forset Close. With the Odles gone away, the Estate moved ahead with their plans for demolition and redevelopment. David had to supervise the quick packing up of all the Odles' effects—books, furniture and linen, all to go into storage. In November 1938, 32 Queen's Terrace was razed to the ground. The local policeman, a friend of theirs, wrote to them that it was a 'pitiful' sight.

Shaken by the loss of their home, Dorothy and Alan came back to London in the following summer and took rooms for a time in a similar house : 'Our pig-in-a-poke turns out to be rather nice in a dilapidated way, same period as 32', in Boundary Road, about half a mile from Queen's Terrace, down the hill towards Kilburn. But there was nothing permanent available at a price they could afford.

The war now seemed imminent. It had not been the most propitious moment for the collected edition of *Pilgrimage* to appear. The edition proved an absolute failure, the royalty statement in 1939 showing a deficit of £4 on the advance of £30. A mere 699 volumes had been sold, and only a few hundred unbound sheets to the American publishers. 'It looks as though they were right,' said Dorothy, 'and *Pilgrimage* is finished . . . Certainly they will not handle the small volume I've been at work on. I shall finish the whole, if I can, and leave it to take its posthumous chance. Meanwhile I must turn to other work.'

At this juncture, Ford Madox Ford's *The March of Literature* was published in England. In it Ford referred to her as a 'great' novelist, the 'most distinguished exponent of English realism', and he then proceeded to state that 'the chief characteristic of this group is an extreme, an almost Flemish, minuteness of rendering of objects and situations perceived . . . Proust carried this tendency to almost the limits of profitable elaboration and was rewarded with a measure of world fame. That the work of Miss Richardson, less wilfully elaborate and much more verbally beautiful, should meet with a complete world neglect is an amazing phenomenon.'

The evacuation from London had begun, with hordes of people jamming the London termini and the roads to the west. If the Odles were to find a Cornish shack, they must hurry; or they would be homeless for a time. Dorothy was now sixty-six and Alan fifty-one. Powys had urged them to come to live near Phyllis and himself in North Wales; and the architect Clough Williams Ellis who had built the neo-Italianate village of Port Meirion had asked them 'to accept, as a present, one of the Italianate villas'; but now that Queen's Terrace was gone, only Cornwall felt like home.

Eventually they managed to get a lift in an A.R.P. car as far as Salisbury; but even from here the trains to the west were impossibly crowded. So they stayed for several days at a commercial hotel by the railway bridge: lucky to get a room there, though their room shook at night because of the trains hurtling past on the viaduct above them.

As they waited for the first rush of people to the west to grow less, they walked about Salisbury, its quiet old streets blocked incongruously by milling crowds and traffic and soldiery, and 'only the cathedral, its Close and precincts retained their ancient serenity'.

In Dorothy's view, this war had been inevitable. 'Was there ever, in the world's history,' she wrote, 'a winter holding so much . . . *fear* and suffering? Yet who, if he had the power, and insight to match, would call off this titanic struggle? *Agreed*, that this is a Capitalistic war. *Agreed*, that it is a war to get, or keep, the upper hand. *Agreed*, that the capitalistic Allies stress money and that the Germans and the Russians stress imponderibilia, believe in the possibility of unanimity and in a socialistic New Jerusalem built by force. Both, equally, exploit. Neither, at its best, can produce anything more than an improved civilization, baths, button pressing, diluted spoon-fed culture for everyman. But the Teutons . . . don't know the meaning of the responsibility born of freedom from pressures, don't know the range and vigour of unwritten laws . . . This titanic struggle has a shining core (whatever the motive in high places): the willingness of the people to endure all things and risk all for freedom. The refusal of the Englishman and the Frenchman to accept coercion. This fundamental . . . insistence on decency of behaviour, may somehow be linked with a slowness and carelessness in cleaning up the mess at home (a business in which the Germans and Scandinavians, *deedy* people with more "character" than "temperament", have always been ahead of us) but is nevertheless their diamond . . . '

Dorothy and Alan reached Trevone in time to rent 'one half of an ex-golf-links shanty . . . divided by a wooden partition from the other half'; and the unremitting noise of the evacuees in the other half made it difficult for the Odles to work. Not that Dorothy had much hope of finishing the last part of *Pilgrimage*. For some time the manuscript had been gathering dust on the latest of the small tables on

L

which she always wrote in the somewhat cramped, *ex tempore* conditions that still suited her best. Alan was still working at his Rabelais, and taking his daily walk on the cliffs, at a pace that made the local children nickname him Mr. Faster. He was shabbier than ever in his 'old mac ... patched and patched and patched with adhesive tape, a battered hat and a home-made sling holding together ... his cargo of drift-wood'.

Dorothy, wishing to give any time that she could spare to the war effort, took on voluntary work as secretary-cum-accountant to a 'distraught farmer' harassed beyond measure by wartime red tape. She also offered continual hospitality to American soldiers and airmen stationed nearby, most of them posted here on their way to the front. Several of these young Americans became attached to the Odles. Young people, it seemed, were drawn to this ageing couple whose outlook had remained fresh.

One day in the local teashop Dorothy got into conversation with a young American airman whose surname, it transpired, was Daniel. He was none other than the long-absent son of her first London friends and mentors, Charles and Florence Daniel, through whom Dorothy had been introduced to that world of eccentric intellectuals, cranks and mystics, presided over by Mary Everest Boole, who is mentioned by name in *Pilgrimage*, and whose collected works Daniel kept in print well into the thirties. Florence (the 'F.E.W.' to whom Dorothy had dedicated *Revolving Lights*) had herself written in 1921 a book, *Are Women Monkey-Minded?*, setting forth the argument that the brain of woman is physiologically different from man's—in fact, superior. Acknowledging her debt to Mrs. Boole, she wrote : 'Women's intuition is no vague, mysterious power, but a mental faculty—a method of inference—strong in her, while weak in most men, because of her age-long practice in it.'

Young Daniel was 'pathetically moved at finding a sort of relative'; and for Dorothy this meeting with him brought back her beginnings in London, and her impressionableness of those days, that had led her to explore so many sects and philosophies. Her subsequent writing, and her beliefs and her mysticism, stemmed from that time. She had kept her searching, positive approach, still believing in the essential goodness of people and of human life. 'Is it not the idealistic progressionists and evolutionists and perfectionists', she wrote, 'who are dismayed by the present unexampled horrors, to the point of "despairing of civilization"?'

Florence Daniel had been dead for twenty years, but Dorothy still sometimes heard from Charles, and she wrote to him, reproaching him for not having given her news of his son. The young man was now posted, by another coincidence, to Calne in Wiltshire, that place Dorothy had 'haunted in the nineties' when her long-dead sister Alice was working as governess to the Harris family. Dorothy still had some acquaintances there, and she wrote a few letters of introduction for young Daniel.

Alice had died peacefully in her sleep some thirty years before; and in March 1941 Kate Batchelor had a similar quiet passing, having contracted pneumonia after flu. Dorothy was stunned by this loss. It made her feel absurdly young and unprotected, she wrote, to have lost 'my dear old Kate' who 'was far from solemn and never disapproving, was indeed, from the first, too indulgent . . . like my undeserved parents'.

Harry Badcock, her 'old dentist man', to whom she had dedicated *Oberland*, had retired several years before to Walsham-le-Willows in Norfolk where he had bought a pleasant cottage for himself and his sister. He now wrote to Dorothy asking her to look out for a place for them near her and Alan, for the duration.

Instinctively her old evasiveness reasserted itself. She wrote back suggesting the south coast of Cornwall as less bleak than their northern shore. 'I can't see him down here, where there is no social centre, and no gentlepeople as he understands the term.' In the event, the Badcocks went instead to Jamaica.

Very occasionally Dorothy found time to write what she envisaged as the last chapter-volume of *Pilgrimage*, each volume being 'a single chapter of an unfinished whole'.

This volume, *March Moonlight*, if ever it was finished, would complete the design as she had originally conceived it. So it began by covering the years, from 1908, of Miriam's return to Switzerland, followed by her break away from the drudgery of her Wimpole Street job, and then her attempt to make her way as a writer, but still with little success. Once again, however, Dorothy had to put aside her own writing; and weeks, and finally years passed, without a page of *March Moonlight* being written. Meanwhile she had been prevailed upon to sell outright to Knopf the American copyright of *Pilgrimage*. Knopf had approached 'Dent, who own rights, about the nuisance of keeping detailed accounts, and sending detailed statements of very small sales, and got him to persuade me to sell out for £30 down, which I gladly did. He is a *lad*, that Knopf.'

The Odles' financial position was now helped in another way. Twice previously her admirers, some of them eminent people, had tried to secure for her a small Civil List pension, and both times they had been turned down, first by Ramsay Macdonald and the second time by Baldwin, who preferred more highly-coloured fiction: he was the enthusiastic patron of *Precious Bane*. But now a third time her partisans, headed by Richard Church, succeeded, and she was allotted a Civil List pension of £100. Another unexpected benefit came from the Estate of Violet Hunt, who died in 1942, leaving Dorothy, as a residuary legatee, the sum of £550. There was also some income from a Trust Fund set up by Bryher for deserving authors. So Dorothy could now begin to put aside some money each year against the possibility of her dying before Alan. She was still tormented by the anxiety that he might be left without enough to live on.

In 1942 she had a letter from Benjamin Grad, who was in an internment camp in France. He asked her 'on behalf of his younger fellow-internees for English books, Grammars, Dictionaries, Text Books and Anthologies'; also a Welsh Bible. He too, undiscouraged by age and disappointments, had kept his intellectual eagerness.

His son David was in the Army, and stationed in the Near East; and Dorothy, writing to Benjamin, devised a code for giving him news of his son's whereabouts, David becoming 'the shepherd's son' in this private cipher.

Veronica was running a hostel in Streatham for old people bombed out of their houses in the early part of the war. At the height of the blitz, these old people had been evacuated from London; whereupon Veronica, instead of closing down the hostel, took in young families who had lost their homes in the bombing.

In 1944 Dorothy brushed the dust off the manuscript of *March Moonlight*, having barely touched it for five years. Slowly she began to work on it again. She was now in her seventies; but the end of the war was distantly in sight; and she managed to find another surge of energy and hopefulness.

Old age, she wrote to a friend, offers compensations. 'For side by side with loss are gains that take one by surprise. For one thing, with relatively nothing ahead, one comes in, so to speak, to all one's investments . . . the whole of one's life, finished and complete, comes into one's hands for re-realization. And this past, sometimes described as reared up and staring one in the face, is misrepresented in being called "unalterable".'

She and Alan both felt, despite the horrors of the war and its doubtful aftermath, that they would rather be alive now than in any other period of history. He was still working hard at his Rabelais. He had aged a little, and his hair was turning grey, but he still kept up his long walks on the cliffs. There was nothing left of his old cynicism, but only 'a certain "detachment" (of a kind that is entirely the reverse of indifference)'. His kindliness and deep interest in people made them warm to him, 'from the yokels and visiting gypsies up to, or down to . . . the local grandees'. She herself was often unwell and in pain, but she managed to keep it from Alan, to spare him anxiety.

Wells also was ill, and despondent. He had lived to acknowledge the failure of many of his ideals of progress by scientific and rational means: a defeat that he now attributed to modern man's inability to adapt to his environment. His pessimism, becoming as extreme as his former optimism, was expressed in his last published work, *Mind at the End of its Tether* (1945). Man, he wrote, having lost control of the forces he himself had created, was doomed.

Dorothy was still devoted to her old enemy and lover: 'poor little Kipps . . . poor little H.G. So sound in science—though not always up-to-date—and in every other way so lost'; but she declined a friend's offer to put her up in London so that she could be near Wells in his last illness. Her place was with Alan. But presently Wells wrote to tell her that 'thanks to disobeying my doctors and nurses in every possible way, I am now in rude health. Apart from gout (well-deserved, thank God!) and bores, I have no afflictions.' The improvement was only temporary. 'To the end he never liked to admit he was so ill as really to need a nurse'. In August 1946 he died.

The atomic cataclysm and the end of the war, had seemed to Dorothy a turning point in history. 'Amidst all the agonies and all the overwhelming difficulties, one question perpetually echoes to and fro: is humanity at last prepared to become a single family? Compulsion through fear of the consequences of any other course is a sad motive, but may in the end help to reveal unsuspected deeper motives. In any case it would seem that the era of padded comfortable life on the promenade deck without a thought for the engine-room and fo'castle is now definitely over.'

There was now the possibility of a French edition of *Pilgrimage*. Over the years a number of foreign publishers had begun negotiations for the rights, including a Barcelona firm that had tried to brave Franco's ban on the work for its 'social subversiveness and atheism', and for whom Dorothy had written in 1943 the very scant, evasive autobiographical 'Data for Spanish Publisher'. But to date there was, apart from the English and American editions, 'only a strange little *Pointed Roofs* in JAPANESE all preface and footnotes and glossary, very pretty to look at'.* However, in the years immediately following the war there were signs of a resurgence of interest from places as distant as India, and

* Duckworth had contracted in August 1933 with the Japanese publishing firm of Kenkyusha for this translation of *Pointed Roofs*.

Dorothy began to receive letters and inquiries from scholars all over the world.

Benjamin Grad, released from his internment camp in France, but worn and aged by his experience, made his way back to England, and one day he turned up on the doorstep of the house in Edinburgh where Veronica was now living with their married daughter. Happily the old couple were reunited.

But presently his spirit of restless searching revived, and he took a job in Paris again, with the European Central Inland Transport Organization. The age limit of sixty was waived in his case, because they found him so able. 'Tragic, though,' wrote Dorothy, 'that he should be driven in old age from the land of his adoption. Thank heaven he likes the work.' Veronica also now returned to her old job as warden of the hostel at Streatham.

Even in old age, these three people had kept their dedication. To a writer friend in America whose health had broken down, Dorothy wrote that she couldn't help attributing this illness to the friend's having given up writing. For herself any prolonged abstinence from writing still 'plays havoc with my well-being'. She was working again on *March Moonlight* : 'any scrap of time plus strength I've had these last years goes to try to finish *Pilgrimage*.' The end was in sight, if only her strength could hold out, as she advanced towards her eighties.

The French publisher Fontaine, who had taken an option on *Pilgrimage*, failed to find a suitable translator, and the project fizzled out; but Dorothy shrugged off such disappointments.* Three successive instalments of *March Moonlight* were published in *Life and Letters*, under the heading of 'Work in Progress', in April, May and November 1946.

'Surely what fiction, at its best, can do,' she wrote at this time, as a corollary to her views on old age, 'is to arrange data, truths in their real relationship by a process of selection. Like an artist making a picture. Something akin

* The first French translation of *Pilgrimage* was the Mercure de France edition of *Pointed Roofs* (*Toits Pointus*, 1965, translated by Marcelle Sibon).

happens to us all as we get on in life. We see data of experience no longer chronologically, but rearranged in their true sequence. The past comes at last to life, transformed, rearranged, immortal.'

In old age, she found herself more than ever in sympathy with young people. In 1947 she had a first visit from the grandchildren of Wells, who were evidently very much drawn to the Odles ; and in turn these young people seemed to her 'alive and aware beyond any but a very few of the last post-war young people . . . Most of the youngsters we meet today . . . are in no sense materialistic, nor imprisoned in any one of the psychological "isms". They have escaped both a misrepresented Darwinism, and a dogmatic Freudianism. A paradox it is, in this externally more and more mechanized age.' She found it heartening too that so many of the old barriers of class and convention, that had persisted through the thirties, were now being levelled.

In the following year she was amazed to receive from Wells's daughter-in-law an enormous parcel containing all the letters and notes that she had ever written to him and to Jame—in spite of his usual habit of destroying private letters. Re-reading some of these fifty-year-old letters attacking his views and his books, and arguing ideas of her own, she noticed ruefully 'the immense difference in clear thought and vivid statement, between those written before I even knew how to cook an egg, and those sent after I had the ceaseless preoccupation of housekeeping ; plus writing pot-boilers and other things. But I do not regret ; oh no.'

It saddened her that several years later, following a visit from a writer who was preparing a biography of Wells, and to whom she spoke frankly, the Wells relations stopped visiting her. One of her remarks, which was quoted in this book, had displeased them ; so that they were 'now ostracizing me for "making out H.G. to be a very unpleasant person"'.

But Alan was still her great concern. To Savage, she wrote in 1947 : 'I'm quite a bit older than you, Harry boy. Tell it, however, not in Gath, neither publish it in the Streets of Ascalon. Anyway, don't tell Alan. The poor darling will have to know in good time that I am about to leave him to fend for himself.'

Then, one morning in February 1948, Alan set out for his usual walk. The weather was uncertain; and he hesitated, looking in on Dorothy, who was cooking in the kitchen, before he went out ... 'It was Alan's day for going into Padstow to change our library books. We had collected the books, discussed the weather, mild and overcast, and he was off through the porch and I into the kitchen. I heard him come back—something left behind? No; he came down through the hall, along the passage and as far as the kitchen door. Glancing up, I met a look so penetrating that it stayed my saucepan-stirring hand. In the way one says something for the sake of saying something, he said, smiling: "D'you think it's *cold?*" I have since wondered whether he wanted to be dissuaded from going. But never in thirty years have I succeeded in dissuading him, when not feeling too well, from keeping to his routine. I think it was a half-conscious intimation ... We again discussed, looked at windows, decided there was a lift, and he went. Toward the top of our hill he was seen, by the young hedger with whom he always passed the time of day, to stagger and fall prone ...

'No one about. Within a minute or two there came, as if summoned, the Padstow district nurse on her bicycle, the policeman who lives at the top of the hill, a friend of ours in a hired car and another friend, walking, who at once telephoned to the doctor, telling him Alan had fainted. He, poor little man, overworked and none too well himself, demurred, but was finally persuaded to come. The friend in the car came down for me. They laid him, on the hedger's long coat, upon the grass verge. A car, the doctor. Getting up from my knees I made way. He bent down, put a hand inside the unfastened clothing, stood back and said indignantly: "He's dead. *I* can't do anything."

'The police waived the law of mortuary and he was brought home. Nurse, though it was not her business but that of a local woman, asked to be allowed to attend to him. The young hedger, saying bitterly "I knew him", asked to be allowed to help her. Everyone loved him ...

'The Coroner waived the law of inquest, helped by the doctor, who, without any sort of examination, invented a certificate : "Heart-failure" . . . A local friend, retired M.D. . . . diagnoses deep-seated lung trouble producing a sudden internal haemorrhage . . .

' . . . in the very midst of the first overwhelming blow, there fell from my heart a burden oppressing it for years past, the unbearable prospect of leaving him alone and helpless . . . '

Through the next months, the nights were unbearable for Dorothy. She had always liked the dark, but now she needed night lights. There were none to be bought in Trevone ; so she wrote to her friend Peggy Kirkaldy, who found her some in Colchester.

In June, Veronica came down to stay with her, and it was a happy reunion, Veronica seeming unchanged 'apart from white hair', so that it was as if they were 'right back in Bloomsbury days'. She came again in December, with Benjamin—'Amabel and Michael . . . for ten days, putting up nearby' ; and the three old friends were together : 'So it has been, after all, a real Christmas.'

By now she could do without the night lights, which she gave away to young mothers in the village. On Christmas Eve this bereaved and tired old woman had received from Powys the urgent message : ' . . . you must *not turn from your Pilgrimage*'s Fruition or drop your staff and scrip !'

So she pressed on, trying to complete her work, and still taking a keen interest in everything around her, despite 'an intermittent longing to return to England' from Cornwall. She would have liked, she said, to visit in London every corner she 'was ever in, except St. John's Wood. That region remains sacred and untouchable.'

In Trevone a local girl with a talent for writing had shyly approached her for advice, and Dorothy had encouraged the girl and was regularly reading and commenting on her work. Other aspirant writers sent her manuscripts and begged her opinion, which she always gave. There were letters from various scholars including one 'from a professor at work upon an article for Encyclopaedia Britannica who gets near to asking the colour of my grandmother's eyes'. She was also coaching a boy in essay writing for his School Certificate examination.

In 1949 she heard that her sister Jessie—that indomitable, bright Harriett who is one of the most attractive characters in *Pilgrimage*—had fallen on hard times in Texas, partly through her husband's illness. Dorothy, anxious to help her, tried to get round the Bank of England currency restrictions preventing her from sending money to her sister. When this failed, she enlisted the help of Knopf in trying to sell the one manuscript that she had kept, *Pointed Roofs*, but there were maddening delays ; so she tried another means. She had some old Devon lace, a family heirloom, and she thought there might be a market for it in America. But meanwhile Jessie had managed to stave off disaster by selling her car, 'a sacrifice almost comparable', Jessie wrote in her old, amused way, 'to losing a child'. She was another one unchanged and undiminished by many vicissitudes.

In this same year, Dorothy was delighted to receive a visit from the grandchildren of her old Harley Street employer Peyton Baly. Of Badcock, still alive and well, settled again in his Norfolk village and writing to her regularly 'in an unchanged hand', she had first-hand news when some friends of hers met him at a guest house. Never, they said, had they 'met anyone more interested in everything, or more interesting'. They were full of enthusiasm for this old man of eighty-four who was still tremendously alive, sawing wood and working in the landlady's garden. Dorothy was greatly touched by these tributes to her 'old dear'.

She herself had a suitor, a retired doctor whose wife had died not long ago. Though she gave him no encouragement, he let his intentions be known to all the village, by leaving a note scribbled for her along the top of her *Daily Telegraph* on her porch, on a morning when at least four people called before she took in the newspaper.

In 1951 she was still struggling, through an attack of 'flu, to write *Pilgrimage*, 'to which only recently I have got back in the hope of finishing it during my seventy-ninth year soon to be entered upon'. The label 'stream of consciousness' still worried her. To an interviewer at this time, she said: 'Stream of consciousness is a muddle-headed phrase. It's not a stream, it's a pool, a sea, an ocean. It has depth and greater depth and when you think you have reached its bottom there is nothing there, and when you give yourself up to one current you are suddenly possessed by another.'

The circulation of *Pilgrimage*, she noted, had 'doubled within the past year'. But in the spring of 1952, she wrote that 'this year, ever since the curtain rose upon the outward scene, I have felt disinclined to do anything but stare, and potter out and sniff the perfumed air. This may be the result of entering my eightieth year.' Six months later, however, she sounded more herself, writing: 'Just upon eighty, I still feel astonishment over the fact, consciously discovered in solitude, at the age of three, of there being anything anywhere, and still look forward . . .'

Pilgrimage Evalued

The technique invented by Dorothy Richardson has become familiar to us through all those later writers who knowingly or not have derived something from her. It is hard for us today to grasp how difficult and strange her way of writing first appeared. Those early reactions of readers and critics, with their inevitable misunderstandings of her work, have dimmed her reputation to this day.

Some of her seeming limitations—occasional prosiness or blurred characterization, lack of compression or selection, or too much—these are part of her method, and therefore part of the cumulative effect of *Pilgrimage*.

The method was evolved to express her vision in the new world of the twentieth century with its changing ways and attitudes. A new kind of voice was needed : not specifically a woman's voice, but one expressing all the awareness and self-doubt of modern people in a world where traditional beliefs had been called into question.

She created, therefore, through her narrator Miriam just such a voice and viewpoint, taking nothing for granted, expressing nothing in the conventional or accepted way. It was a method belonging to the new age but stemming from the nineteenth-century analytical approach. It was closely equivalent to Impressionism in painting.

Pilgrimage might be called the first full-scale Impressionist novel. As never before in a novel, Dorothy Richardson attempted to show us what we really perceive, not what we accept as reality according to certain conventions. In her descriptions and also in depicting emotion and thought, her novel portrays reality as continual movement and fluctuation. To let this reality filter through as lucidly as possible, the novelist must keep his own voice from obtruding—from commenting, summarizing, drawing hard lines of de-marcation of character or incident—just as the Impressionist painters had rejected the convention of firm outline. Similarly there could be no arbitrary 'plot' imposed on the material, distorting the truth. If a novel were made alive enough by capturing the flow of reality, then its immediacy should be more exciting than any contrived plot.

Pilgrimage is literally a 'motion picture', in its view of the ceaseless fluctuation of people's lives, minds and hearts, and in its prismatic analysis of perceptions into their elements. But its author was searching as well for something constant and essential underlying the continual movement in beings or objects. 'There was something in matter that had not yet been found out.' The search for reality, in this new writing, was also an attempt to rediscover meanings and truths that the twentieth-century mind could no longer take on trust. This is the search that gives the novel its title *Pilgrimage* and its central theme.

The path subdivides as Miriam tries various worlds of experience, personal, spiritual and intellectual. Intellect, for Dorothy Richardson, was a lesser thing than intelligence. And yet, despite her mistrust of thought, as tending to obviate awareness, there is probably too much thinking in *Pilgrimage*. The intellectual searchings are the least effective part of the book, though they do recreate for us vividly the intellectual ferment of that time, with its many new beliefs and discoveries : an atmosphere of eager aspiration. Whether or not one rejected, with Miriam, Darwin's theories of natural selection, and Wells's concept of man as a magician-scientist, a Prospero striving to become a kind of universal stage-manager, still in that exciting new age it was difficult not to believe in some kind of progress.

In most of the theories and sects that Miriam explores in the novel, she finds something valid ; but none of them holds her in the end. Any organized set of beliefs, she finds, however untrammelled at first, will finally create its own conventions and prejudices. All of them blinker the vision. So progress must come through individual growth towards awareness and expression. Miriam, shedding her early intellectual snobbery, comes to believe that in every human consciousness is latent a fuller awareness. All the wasted and unfulfilled intelligences, kept down by social injustice and conventional mentality, must be set free. Industrialization with its side-effects of mass-mind and mass-entertainments of a deadening sort, was an enemy of progress.

The highest aim of art was, then, to illuminate consciousness. Imagination is, for her, again, a heightened awareness, enabling any person to project himself into the lives of other people, and into the reality of objects. That anything exists—the most ordinary object—is continually a marvel to her, and none of this wonder can be taken for granted. Increasingly she longs to be alone, with her vision unimpeded by people.

In time we see her learning to manage people better, and coming more out of herself, but she always escapes from close attachments. The *Dimple Hill* volume is a story of betrayal and sadness—except that we are left in some doubt as to who is the betrayer. It almost seems that Miriam caused it to turn out unhappily, so that she might escape again into solitude.

The characters of the novel, presented to the reader as Miriam sees them, often have the blurred, inconsistent, oblique quality of people as we ourselves see them in real life. Certain characters come and go and reappear as unexpectedly or inexplicably as in life. Amabel and the Quaker farmer Richard are neither of them wholly 'satisfactory' characters by ordinary novel standards. But there is nothing wrong with Miriam's observation. She can sum up a character at first meeting, in a few words.

People are, in Miriam's life and in the world of this novel, ultimately not too satisfactory. It is a novel much taken up with seeming failure in relationships; beginning with Miriam's guilt over her parents; her own youthful awkwardness as a person, and her sense of the clutter of most relationships, since people, like thinking, tend to block one's vision and one's sense of reality.

People also, in a world of fluctuation, change constantly. Everyone is going a different way, each with his own frames of reference, no two people speaking quite the same language. Miriam is at once over-generous and wary with people. She never can calculate. She gets hurt because of her honesty and lack of contrivance, the directness that is as much a part of her character as of her vision. She is never possessive. Even in her closest involvements with people she is always at the same time detached. She will let herself be hurt or used, but no one can belong to her for long. Her straightness, and her search for reality, are hard on relationships. Despite her impressionistic view, she fixes very clearly the value of people.

Herself too she sees with a microscopic accuracy : her lack of charity, tolerance and patience, her gracelessness, the shyness that makes her seem aggressive or cold ; her inability to let herself go, her position as an outsider, apart from ordinary human warmth and pleasure. She is different from all the other people in the novel ; and yet, although she is not very beautiful or after the first volumes young, she has a power over people ; they are drawn to her, women and men (from letters we know this was also the case with her creator). Throughout the book, Miriam is much more the beloved than the lover, someone pursued by involvements and commitments, from which she is impelled to break away—thereby hurting herself most of all. The other people want her or need her in various ways, and yet curiously the greater share of intensity is on her side : she is vulnerable, a source of light-energy and emotion of which people are instinctively aware and which draws them to her, to drain these resources of hers. This power is, simply, the magnetic field of her genius.

In Miriam, without making any special claim for her, and showing her as full of doubts and self-denigration, Dorothy Richardson has none the less created that most difficult of all characters to make credible : a genius. Following her growth in intelligence and vision through the successive volumes of *Pilgrimage*, we recognize genius.

In her early days, she judges men harshly. This is part of her youthful intolerance, and later she is less sweepingly dismissive of the mentality of most men. And yet, again she is giving us an accurate picture of an age, still entirely a man's world, when more than today, people's minds went in ruts of conventional sentiments, catch-phrases, prejudices. Miriam's feminism stems from her view that women are less stereotyped in their thinking and more aware than men, and therefore closer to reality. Men tended to a factual, one-dimensional view of the world ; and she was aiming at a comprehensive view of all dimensions at once : the artist's impossible, magical view, in which science and theology, matter and spirit, would be reconciled. The artist, the outsider, could come nearest to containing this unity.

The theme of the artist as outsider, on his lonely path of vision, is an old one, but presented by her without sentimentality or pretension. *Pilgrimage* is a hard book, and the journey undertaken by Miriam is a hard one, with many privations and changes of direction as various paths prove dead ends. It is a pilgrim's life, constantly on the move, and always confirming her view that relationships get in the way of her vision and therefore of reality, that the vision is only to be found in solitude and silence.

So Miriam is essentially an anti-social being. She sees the lights of some comfortable haven—marriage to her employer, called Hancock in the novel, or to Densley, the doctor who courts her—but, however ill and tired and lost she may feel, she must go on her solitary way.

The journey leaves her homeless as well. We follow her migratory life, from one post as a teacher to another, then in London from lodging house to hostel, then a *pension* in Switzerland, a room on a farm. On the one occasion when she tries to make a home of her own with Miss Holland, she fails.

There is guilt in this too, the sense of being an outcast as well as an outsider, the artist's original guilt of being different from everyone else, of seeing people's characters too clearly and cruelly, of lacking the common touch of sympathy that could have saved her mother when she took her on that fatal last trip to the seaside.

Searching to find some resolution of this guilt, and tormented by the image of a shop sign that she associates with her dead mother, she sees that time itself is not apart from the ceaseless fluctuation of experience. The past, as it recurs, is sometimes clearer and more vivid than originally, and new relationships and meanings emerge from it. Out of this experience, Dorothy Richardson evolved her theory of 'horizontal' rather than 'vertical' time, of the past and the present existing in the same stratum, assembled as on the canvas of a painting, if we could but see it.

Pilgrimage, then, is a novel on the many different levels—perception, spirit, intellect, emotion—that Miriam's own life comprises. It is a Renaissance kind of life, and the novel is a soaring attempt at resolution of all these aspirations and ideas. Those friends of her early days in London, with their strange, courageous, cranky ideologies, were right at least in aiming at beliefs comprehensive of every field of thought.

Whether or not *Pilgrimage* works as a novel is ultimately a question for the individual reader; but it is, in its immensity and diversity, a work of cathedral-like magnitude. Only *Ulysses* among modern English novels attempts the same scale of importance. *Pilgrimage* is, in the view of this critic, a flawed but great novel.

How to compare it with Joyce's work? Briefly, there are some immediate points of comparison with Joyce and also with Proust, the two writers with whom her name was formerly linked as a great innovator. Proust and Joyce are less bound than she to absolute reality; and imagination is something more for them than for her. In their different ways, both are romantics, Joyce deviously. *Ulysses* and *A la recherche du temps perdu* are both novels of great emotionality. *Pilgrimage* is a more controlled work, concerned above all with the human spirit rather than with human emotions. Romanticism at its best, as in these other two writers, is the bias of feeling. Although it may be a distortion of reality, it can give a work of art its final stamp of greatness.

Proust is more obviously than Joyce a romantic, with the highly-charged longings, wishful thinking, and dreams of nobility and chivalry we find in his work, although he also explores disappointments, self-doubt and disillusionment—but even disillusionment, in Proust, is rich fare. Proust meticulously records impressions and details, but reflected in his depths of sensibility, a kind of *cathédrale engloutie*, creating a work of beauty not entirely real.

Emotional sensibility is notable too in the writings of Virginia Woolf and Katherine Mansfield, who followed Proust, Richardson and Joyce, and whose work was on a smaller scale, but also enriched by the bias of emotion. Virginia Woolf was an intellectual, but she heightened the emotional content of her work by her way of telescoping her characters' lives and the passage of time; as did also Katherine Mansfield.

Virginia Woolf had a rarer, more poetic imagination than Dorothy Richardson, but she was also more limited in her range. She portrayed the highest sensibility, but little below it. Her life, like her art, was a more enclosed, restricted one than Dorothy Richardson's. Her emotional difficulties were great, but she lived in the shelter of the Bloomsbury group, and a marriage which kept her within that set. The Bloomsbury group, though among themselves their lives were often strange and unconventional, were an enclosed society, set apart from the commonplace world. In Virginia Woolf's novels, correspondingly, there is no wide human range as there is in *Pilgrimage*, which encompasses in depth and with understanding such diverse characters as Mrs. Bailey, Michael Shatov, Rachel Mary and H. G. Wilson, as well as Miriam's own consciousness.

Virginia Woolf's debt to Dorothy Richardson may be clearly seen. Her own view, in 1925, of the ideal novel— that if a novelist 'could write what he chose, there would be no plot, no comedy, no tragedy, no love interest or catastrophe in the accepted sense'—exactly described the method of *Pilgrimage*; but Virginia Woolf could not quite bring herself to practise such an absolute, austere truthfulness. Five years before, in her *Writer's Diary*, she had questioned the absoluteness of Joyce and Dorothy Richardson in following this method : 'I suppose the danger is the damned egotistical self, which ruins Joyce and Richardson to my mind : Is one pliant and rich enough to provide a wall for the book from oneself without its becoming, as in Joyce and Richardson, narrowing and restricting?' Virginia Woolf, unlike the author of *Pilgrimage*, was prepared to intervene, as the writer consciously adding certain elements to enliven what readers might otherwise find too bare a reality: 'My hope is that I've learnt my business sufficiently now to provide all sorts of entertainments.'

She followed Dorothy Richardson not only in her mode of writing, but also in the feminism of her novels, where she depicted the acute sensibility of Mrs. Dalloway and other women characters transcending the more dulled awareness of the men round them. It might have been Miriam writing this entry from Virginia Woolf's *Diary* in 1919: 'The male atmosphere is disconcerting to me. Do they distrust one? despise one? . . . I think what an absolute precipice cleaves asunder the male intelligence, and how they pride themselves upon a point of view which much resembles stupidity.' Elizabeth Bowen later wrote of Virginia Woolf's 'obsession . . . that women were being martyrized humanly, inhibited creatively, by the stupidities of a man-made world'. It is exactly the viewpoint that had been expressed from the outset of *Pilgrimage*.

Virginia Woolf did acknowledge, in her review of *Revolving Lights* in 1923, that Dorothy Richardson had been the first novelist to create a method and a language for expressing the feminine consciousness: 'There is no one word, such as romance or realism, to cover, even roughly, the works of Miss Dorothy Richardson. Their chief characteristic . . . is one for which we still seek a name. She has invented . . . a sentence . . . of a more elastic fibre than the old, capable of stretching to the extreme, of suspending the frailest particles, of enveloping the vaguest shapes. Other writers of the opposite sex have used sentences of this description and stretched them to the extreme. But there is a difference. Miss Richardson has fashioned her sentence consciously, in order that it may descend to the depths and investigate the crannies of Miriam Henderson's consciousness. It is a woman's sentence, but only in the sense that it is used to describe a woman's mind by a writer who is neither proud nor afraid of anything she may discover in the psychology of her sex... Her discoveries are concerned with states of being and not with states of doing. Miriam is aware of "life itself"; of the atmosphere of the table rather than of the table; of the silence rather than of the sound. Therefore she adds an element to her perception of things which has not been noticed before, or, if noticed, has been guiltily suppressed... Miriam Henderson points too didactically... But, be that as it may, here we have... Miss Richardson proving that the novel is not hung upon a nail and festooned with glory, but, on the contrary, walks the high road, alive and alert, and brushes shoulders with real men and women.'

This was high praise, but Virginia Woolf never re-affirmed it. In all her critical essays that make up the several collected volumes, there are only a few references to Dorothy Richardson, her attitude towards her appearing somewhat grudging. She was, however, even more grudging in her view of Katherine Mansfield: 'Her mind is a very thin soil, laid an inch or two deep upon very barren rock... She writes badly too.' *Ulysses* she dismissed as 'an illiterate, underbred book... the book of a self-taught working man'; and she found Lawrence 'airless, confined'. It is not surprising, then, that she never adequately expressed her debt to Dorothy Richardson. Had she been more generous, she might have helped to redress the balance of which Powys commented to Dorothy: 'She is acclaimed on both sides of the Atlantic, a household name, when you are forgotten.' In the event, a detailed critical study of Virginia Woolf's work, published in 1949, could express the view that Virginia Woolf 'did supremely well what no one else has attempted to do'.

Joyce's romanticism, setting him like these other con-temporaries apart from Dorothy Richardson, is none the less powerful for being half-hidden in his cabbalistic patterns of language, half-disguised behind the patter and the cynicism. *Ulysses* is surely, in its emotional vehemence and bitterness, in its transfiguration of the crude and the seedy, one of the most romantic of all novels. The same emotionality lies behind many of the stories, and *A Portrait*

169

of the Artist as a Young Man. And the very names and titles, *Stephen Hero*, Stephen Daedalus: these are romantic conceptions; and it would not have been startlingly inappropriate if he had called his work *A Portrait of a Young Romantic*, for all the work's startings and stoppings of emotion, its aspirations threatened or besmirched, its special pleading of pain and excitement and bitter resentment that underlay nearly everything Joyce wrote. A modern romantic, however, could not write like the old ones. Too much was now known and too many disillusionments had been discovered. The 'self-doubting voice of the twentieth century' had to be expressed in a seemingly bitter view of life, in mocking and self-mocking doggerel. But still the driving emotion in the work often surges past the other controls.

Legend is another romantic ploy. Proust creates an aura of legend about the Guermantes; and Joyce, with his odd rhythms and narrative patterns, sometimes doggerel, sometimes like a border ballad or Celtic saga, or a pseudo-mediaeval pastiche, gives to certain passages a looming, abstract quality, magnifying them beyond reality.

Ulysses has in common with *Pilgrimage* a magnitude of scope, and its exploration of the interior world and vision of its central character; and, more superficially, the power of its author to evoke a city, Dublin, as a living entity, like Dorothy Richardson's London. But *Pilgrimage* has no underlying romanticism and offers no legend. It has instead its unbiased and luminous honesty, its clarity of vision uncluttered by linguistic tricks.

'By imposing very strict limitations on herself,' May Sinclair wrote of *Pilgrimage*, 'she has brought her art, her method, to a high pitch of perfection . . . Miss Richardson has only imposed on herself the conditions that life imposes on us all. And if you are going to quarrel with those conditions, you will not find her novel satisfactory . . . In identifying herself with this life, which is Miriam's stream of consciousness, Miss Richardson produces her effect of being the first, of getting closer to reality than any of our novelists who are trying so desperately to get close . . . It is as if no other writers had ever used their senses so purely or with so intense a joy in their use.'

Is it, however, this realism—as opposed to the romanticism of Proust, Joyce and Virginia Woolf—that has caused *Pilgrimage* to be forgotten while those other works are still read? Did Dorothy Richardson's over-scrupulous honesty and intelligence deprive her work of an aura, a personality, that would preserve it through time? Her honesty, luminous sometimes, is at other times almost painfully flat, undercutting the emotion that is also considerable in the work, but never allowed to get out of hand. The book, for all its lyrical moments, remains bare and spare and hard, never rich and rare. It is religiously plain, as befits a Pilgrimage whose purposes, as well as aesthetic, are spiritual, so that our critical frames of reference falter a little. The book is a novel and also something more : a work with some quality like that of Bunyan, whom she greatly admired and from whom she took the title of her book.

Viewing it as a spiritual as well as fictional work, altering one's responses and one's focus of judgment, one finds in *Pilgrimage* a light, an intensity, a visionary quality that to a degree compensate for its lack of an imagination that these other novelists have. For Dorothy Richardson's imagination was too much bound by reality. She gave us life itself complete, but unadorned and untransfigured in spite of the visionary moments in the book.

It has a realism, almost needless to say, beyond what now commonly passes as 'realism' in the novel but, being only the shallowest surface observation, comes nowhere near reality. She gives us instead, with the continual flow of incident and character, the real complexity of a world of innumerable possibilities and truths, where people go their different ways, all at cross-purposes ; a world in which a pattern of light, or a sudden new angle on a city street, leaps out, immensely and joyfully alive ; a world, then, teeming with all these inanimate lives, like the strange diagram of some mediaeval naturalist ; a world in which—as in that first, recurrent memory of hers as a child in a garden with the flowerbed towering above her—the stature of people in relation to things can be proportionately less; but the pleasures and pain of emotion and the minutest details of relationship are intricately known, and magnified by her awareness of every breath and particle of life.

In December 1953 Rose Odle was summoned urgently by
Dorothy's landlady in Trevone. Dorothy, now eighty, had
been seriously ill with shingles ; and since the illness she had
been restless and disturbed in her manner. Badcock's death
in October had saddened her deeply. Late at night her
landlady would hear her moving about, pacing up and down.
Physically, she still appeared hardy, and she still had her
cold bath each morning.

Dorothy was displeased that Rose—herself frail after a
heart attack—had had to make the journey from Kent.
Moreover, there was no spare bed or bedding in the flat.
But Rose and the landlady brought down a camp bed to the
spare room. The room, scarcely heated, was freezing in this
December cold ; but Rose stayed on for two weeks, trying
to make things more comfortable for Dorothy.

There was a gas pipe, Rose noticed, hanging loose and
partially disconnected. But Dorothy wasn't concerned about
it. After all the years of being practical and capable for Alan
as well as herself, she was finally letting go. She hardly
bothered to eat, and she had certain obsessions that preoccupied her, such as her continual sending of parcels to
people. It was as if, with Alan dead, she had to find other
outlets for her anxious concern. On a table in the spare room
was a large box of brown paper and string for the parcels,
and on the wall above was a large picture, back view, of a
naked baby boy—the sort of picture that a mother might
keep of a son long grown up. It made Rose remember how
Alan had said, half-ironically, half-sadly, that it was a pity
that Dorothy had lost Wells's child.

When Rose expressed concern about a possible gas leak,
Dorothy replied that the Gas Board would do nothing :
it took three months to get anything done. However,
Rose cajoled and bullied them into sending a fitter at once.
He arrived and was horrified when he saw the loose pipe,

telling them it was a wonder they hadn't been blown up.

Rose also had the flat rewired, and had an electric fire fitted in the wall, as otherwise Dorothy in her abstractedness might have walked into it and set herself alight. An electric ring for cooking was also installed, as being safer than the gas.

Even with all these precautions, it now began to seem as though Dorothy couldn't live here alone. The landlady couldn't be constantly on call, in case of an accident. But Dorothy wanted only to stay in this flat, with its associations of Alan, and with the manuscript of the last volume of *Pilgrimage*, still seemingly unfinished, yellowing and gathering dust on the small table where she had always written. On the chimneypiece was the same array of old postcards, the bust of Voltaire that once had cracked but had been carefully mended by David Grad, the photograph of Allinson's portrait of Alan.

Rose would have taken Dorothy to live with her in Kent, but her bungalow was too inaccessible, with its innumerable steps and a steeply sloping garden that set it far back from the road. In any case, even if Dorothy could be persuaded to leave this flat, she would want to stay somewhere nearby.

Rose arranged, at the end of her fortnight, that the District Nurse should call twice a week, and that the doctor should also look in on Dorothy twice weekly. The daily woman would see to meals. Dorothy still kept up the old ritual of tea, a part of the day that she and Alan had especially enjoyed. She would lay the same linen cloth on the table and put out the tea things exactly as of old, even when no one was with her to share the ritual.

As soon as Rose had gone, Dorothy rang up the Dunrovan Hotel at Trevone, and moved there the next day. She could not bear to have her independence curtailed by all these arrangements of nurses, doctors and daily women. But during the next three months, while she was staying at the hotel, her forgetfulness and vagueness increased.

In March Philip Batchelor, her nephew, who was still living in Ealing, had an urgent telephone call from the hotel manager. Dorothy, it seemed, was becoming a nuisance ; other guests were complaining. In the dining-room sometimes she would wander about, absently picking up things from the tables she passed. The manager claimed that the hotel was fully booked for Easter, and she must move out in the next four days.

Batchelor passed this news on to Rose, and together they went down to Trevone. Arriving, they telephoned innumerable nursing homes in Cornwall, but were unable to get Dorothy in anywhere ; till finally a place was found for her in a nursing home at Beckenham, Kent. It would be easier for Rose and friends from London to visit her there.

On the eve of the proposed move from the Dunrovan Hotel, Dorothy had a further setback, and next morning she stayed in her bed, refusing to leave the hotel. But the manager's wife at last persuaded her to go. So Dorothy, with Rose and Philip Batchelor, caught the train, having planned to break their journey that night at Exeter, where they had booked rooms at the Queen's Hotel.

Dorothy, bitterly distressed at leaving Cornwall, was difficult at first on the train journey. But presently some other people came into their compartment. Her old interest in people, and her passion for observing, brought her out of her distress ; and soon she had them all listening rapt to her stories of famous people.

But arriving at Exeter, she had another relapse. Tired, despairing and talking disconnectedly, she retired to her bed at the Queen's Hotel. The other two, fearing that there might be some awkwardness or incident, thought they had better prepare the manager, by telling him that she was a sick woman. She now seemed near collapse, and they wanted to stay for an extra night, but the manager hastily informed them that their rooms had been booked for a conference party arriving the following day, which was Sunday.

Later, while Dorothy was washing, a hotel maid unpacked for her. Dorothy, returning to her room, was confused and alarmed at finding her cases empty, and accused the maid of robbing her. The maid complained irately to the manager.

Meanwhile Rose and Batchelor were sitting in the lounge, where suddenly Dorothy appeared, fully dressed again. She had tried to do her hair in a bun, but long strands of it, thick and still partially golden, had come loose and were hanging down grotesquely.

She walked past them, moving round the lounge with an air of immense, commanding dignity, commenting disdainfully on the décor and the furnishings and pictures. There were other people in the lounge, and everyone was watching her. But such was her dignity, that nobody laughed, or even spoke. There was absolute silence, as she walked out again.

The maid, while unpacking her cases, had also contrived to spill the salts that Dorothy took every morning at nine. Dorothy, in spite of her carelessness about other things, was still firm about hygiene : next morning she wouldn't take the salts that had been scooped up from the carpet.

So Rose set out from the hotel, in the hope of finding a chemist's shop open on Sunday. Near to tears, she walked on for more than a mile, till luckily she found a chemist's open on the outskirts of Exeter. She was back at the hotel just in time to give the salts to Dorothy on the stroke of nine. Whereupon Dorothy sat up and in her old manner and voice said : 'Be patient with my impatience, Rose.' And Rose wept.

So they got her to Beckenham, where the Scots couple who ran the nursing home settled her into a room with two others. The Scotsman, Munro, turned out to be an admirer of Alan's work. But Dorothy, independent as ever, was appalled at the prospect of sharing a room with other patients, and at first she refused, insisting that she must go to an hotel. However, Mrs. Munro assured Rose that they could manage the situation. The doctor would be coming in shortly, to give Dorothy a sedative injection.

On the train journey from Trevone to Exeter, she had seemed to be in pain, twitching away from Batchelor when he tried to adjust her shawl. The doctor at the nursing home diagnosed probable cancer of the shoulder, accounting for this pain ; but it was inoperable.

The fees were low at the nursing home—only £5 per week, though that was soon doubled. The Munros were kind, and Dorothy gradually became reconciled to sharing her room with two other old women. She would even look after them tenderly when they were unwell, or at night if their covers had slipped she would tuck them in again.

For more than a year, however, she did not forgive Rose for having taken her away from Cornwall; and she showed little interest in Rose's visits. There were few other visitors; and those who came, like Owen Wadsworth—the lonely young man of decades ago whom she had set on his journalistic career and who had been 'someone for Alan'— found her sadly changed.

The two other women whose room she shared had many more visitors than she; and she came to envy their good fortune. They in turn resented her habit of telling their visitors that it was time to go. They became so annoyed, that Dorothy had to be transferred to a room on her own; and now she begged to be put back with the other two.

By now she had forgiven Rose. It was 1957, and she was in her eighty-fourth year. On a fine afternoon when Rose came to visit her, she led the way out of the house—not into the neatly laid-out garden but into the wilder little patch of kitchen garden, to sit by a compost heap; and suddenly, in exactly her old tone of remarking that something was good, she exclaimed, probably for the last time in her life, on what a miracle it was that anything existed, and how beautiful the world was, as she gestured round this little wilderness surrounding the compost heap.

She was failing rapidly. Visiting her again on the Friday, 14 June, Rose found her as if already gone away. It was the beginning of the strawberry season; and hopefully Rose had brought strawberries and cream for them to eat in the garden, but Dorothy was past such pleasures. Mrs. Munro, however, said reassuringly that she had seen Dorothy as ill as this before.

On the following Monday morning, 17 June, Rose was awakened by a telephone call. Dorothy was dead.

In Dorothy's handbag was found a note giving certain instructions: among them, that four people should be informed of her death, the four being Rose, Philip Batchelor, Veronica Grad and Veronica's son David. In the hand-bag was also found one letter, which she had obviously kept there for some years—a letter from Veronica Grad.

Later that day, Veronica telephoned Rose, in distress and anguish, to ask her help. In 1917, when Alan had been too poor to afford a wedding ring for Dorothy, the Grads had bought one for them. This ring Veronica now wanted, to wear in memory of her friend. But it seemed at first that she would not have her wish. Dorothy had willed her body to medical research; and already, so soon after her death, the body had been removed to a hospital, no one seemed quite to know where.

Eventually they found this anonymous body in a hospital laboratory—in time for the ring to be removed from the finger and given to Veronica, who wore it till her own death a few years afterwards.

The remaining typescript chapters of the last volume of *Pilgrimage* were now read; and it was seen that Dorothy had succeeded before dying in her aim of completing the circle of her work; bringing it in this last chapter *March Moonlight* (published posthumously in 1967) to the point where Miriam in her Queen's Terrace lodging house meets the strange, lost, shabby, courteous young man—whom we recognize as Alan Odle—and where also she is about to embark on the novel that we, identifying her with her creator, know to be her *Pilgrimage*.

Of *Pilgrimage*, John Cowper Powys had written to her some years before: 'I think your not being allowed by England to devote yourself *to your own work* is the greatest literary disgrace of our time. It makes me feel heart-sick, Dorothy, to think of your having to do all this pot-boiling instead of going on with the next chapter of Miriam . . . yet it has been known that someone like you . . . at two removes from the crowd's comprehension, has touched some nerve . . . that sends forth such hushed awe of recognition that the crowd *has* to take off its hat and think to itself "*numen inest*!" Such things *have* been known—they have—yes, they *have*! but we shall see. Perhaps this recognition will arrive to embarrass and distract you yet . . .'

It had not happened like that.

Bibliography and Sources

NB The abbreviated form given in parenthesis at the end of
    an entry applies to the Source References in the Notes

I   Primary Sources

A   Books by Dorothy M. Richardson

A1 First Editions of *Pilgrimage* (London)
    Pointed Roofs. Duckworth, 1915
    Backwater. Duckworth, 1916
    Honeycomb. Duckworth, 1917
    The Tunnel. Duckworth, 1919
    Interim. Duckworth, 1919
    Deadlock. Duckworth, 1921
    Revolving Lights. Duckworth, 1923
    The Trap. Duckworth, 1925
    Oberland. Duckworth, 1927
    Dawn's Left Hand. Duckworth, 1931
    Clear Horizon. J. M. Dent and The Cresset Press,
        1935
    Dimple Hill: contained in *Pilgrimage*: Collected
                    Edition, 4 vols. J. M. Dent and The
                    Cresset Press, 1938
    March Moonlight: contained in *Pilgrimage*: Collected
                    Edition, 4 vols. J. M. Dent, 1967

A2 Non-fiction (London)
    The Quakers Past and Present. Constable, 1914
    Gleanings from the Works of George Fox. Headley, 1914
    John Austen and the Inseparables. William Jackson,
        1930

B   Essays, Sketches, Stories, Poems and Reviews by
    Dorothy M. Richardson. The basic list of these is
    provided by Joseph Prescott in 'A Preliminary Check-
    list of the Periodical Publications of Dorothy M.
    Richardson', published in *Studies in Honor of John*

Wilcox, ed. A. D. Wallace and W. O. Ross, Wayne State University Press, Detroit, 1958. The following are quoted or referred to in this work:

' "Days with Walt Whitman" ', *Crank: An Unconventional Magazine*, aug. 1906, 259–263 (DMR (M))

'Mr. Clive Bell's Proust', *New Adelphi*, dec. 1928–feb. 1929, 160–162 (DMR(P))

'Novels', *Life and Letters Today*, mar. 1948. 188–192 (DMR(Q))

'Old Age', *Adam*, 1966, 25–26 (DMR(C))

'Peach Harvest', *The Saturday Review*, 19 july 1913, 78–79 (DMR(N))

'A Sussex Auction', *The Saturday Review*, 13 june 1908, 755 (DMR(O))

'Visitor', *Life and Letters*, sep. 1945, 167–172 (DMR (D))

'What's In a Name', *Adelphi*, dec. 1924, 606–609 (DMR(E))

'Women and the Future', *Vanity Fair*, apr. 1924, 39–40 (DMR(F))

'Women in the Arts', *Vanity Fair*, may 1925, 47,100 (DMR(G))

'Yeats of Bloomsbury', *Life and Letters Today*, apr. 1939, 606–609 (DMR(H))

C   Published Autobiographical and Biographical Material

C1   Autobiographical Material
'Beginnings: A Brief Sketch', *Ten Contemporaries: Notes Toward Their Definitive Bibliography* (second series), ed. John Gawsworth (ps. T.I.F. Armstrong) (Joiner and Steele, London, 1933) (Beginnings)
'Data for Spanish Publisher', ed. Joseph Prescott. *The London Magazine*, june 1959, 14–19 (Data)

C2   Biographical Material
Brome, Vincent. 'A Last Meeting with Dorothy

Richardson', *The London Magazine*, june 1959, 26–32 (Brome(A))

Bryher. 'D.R.', *Adam*, 1966, 22–24 (Bryher(A))

Glikin, Gloria. 'Dorothy M. Richardson: The Personal "Pilgrimage"', *Publications of The-Modern-Language-Association-of-America*, dec. 1963, 586–600 (Glikin(A))

Odle, Rose I. 'Dorothy and Alan', *Adam*, 1966, 27–34 Odle(A))

[Prescott, Joseph]. 'Dorothy Miller Richardson', *Encyclopaedia Britannica* (Benton, 1967), XIX, 307 (Prescott(A))

Prescott, Joseph. 'Seven Letters from Dorothy M. Richardson', *The Yale University Library Gazette*, jan. 1959, 102–111 (Prescott(B))

The Times (London), 'Miss Dorothy Richardson, Pioneer Among Novelists', Obituary, 18 june 1957, 13 (Times(A))

Twentieth Century Authors, eds. Stanley J. Kunitz and Howard Haycraft. (H. W. Wilson, New York, 1942), 1169–1170

Wadsworth, P. B. 'My Friendship with D. R.', *Adam*, 1966, 35–40 (Wadsworth)

D   Unpublished Material
The originals of most of these papers and letters are in the Dorothy Richardson Collection at Yale University Library

D1   Miscellaneous unpublished papers and manuscript notes by Dorothy M. Richardson (DMR), mostly undated, including a 'Literary Essay' on her method of writing, and ' "Amende Quincale" for *Adelphi*', correcting some misrepresented statements by DMR quoted by the author of an unspecified article on H. G. Wells. The following are quoted or referred to in this work:
Dorothy M. Richardson. ' "Amende Quincale" for *Adelphi*' (DMR(R))

Dorothy M. Richardson. 'Literary Essay' (DMR(J))
Dorothy M. Richardson. 'Seen from Paradise' (DMR(K))
Dorothy M. Richardson. 'Wanted, the Play Spirit' (DMR(L))

D2 Unpublished letters written by Dorothy M. Richardson (DMR) to the following persons. These letters, some of which are wholly or partially undated, are referred to by the initials of the recipient, in the Source References of this work
John Austen (to JA)
Mrs. John Austen (to Mrs. JA)
Curtis Brown (to CB)
Bernice Elliott (to BE)
David Grad (to DG)
Veronica Grad (to VG)
E. B. C. Jones (to EBCJ)
Peggy Kirkaldy (to PK)
Louise Morgan (to LM)
Rose I. Odle (to RIO)
Ruth Pollard (to RP)
John Cowper Powys (to JCP)
Henry Savage (to HS)
Ruth Suckow (to RS)

D3 Unpublished letters, other than those written by Dorothy M. Richardson (DMR). These letters, some of which are wholly or partially undated, are referred to, in the Source References of this work, by the initials of both sender and recipient
Frances Gale to DMR (FG to DMR)
Veronica Grad to Rose I. Odle (VG to RIO) (These letters, all of which are undated but c. 1957, are numbered 1 to 7)
Veronica Grad to DMR (VG to DMR)
Ernest Hemingway to DMR (EH to DMR)
Jessie A. Hale to Rose I. Odle (JAH to RIO)
Louise Morgan to DMR (LM to DMR)

Rose I. Odle to John Rosenberg (RIO to JR)
Phyllis Playter to Rose I. Odle (PP to RIO)
John Cowper Powys to DMR (JCP to DMR)
Mary Tate to Rose I. Odle (MT to RIO)

II   Secondary Sources

A   Books

Blackstone, Bernard. *Virginia Woolf, A Commentary* (The Hogarth Press, London, 1949) (Blackstone)

Boole, Mary Everest. *The Message of Psychic Science to the World* (C. W. Daniel, London, 1908) (Boole)

Bowen, Elizabeth. *Collected Impressions* (Longmans, London, 1950) (Bowen)

Brome, Vincent. *H. G. Wells* (Longmans, London, 1951)

Bryher. *The Heart to Artemis* (Collins, London, 1963) (Bryher(B))

Daniel, Florence. *Are Women Monkey-Minded?* (C. W. Daniel, London, 1921) (Daniel)

The Dictionary of National Biography: The Concise Dictionary Part II (Oxford University Press, 1916) (DNB)

Dickson, Lovat. *H. G. Wells: His Turbulent Life and Times* (Macmillan, London, 1969) (Dickson)

Ellmann, Richard. *James Joyce* (Oxford University Press, 1959) (Ellmann)

Ford, Ford Madox. *The March of Literature* (Allen & Unwin, London, 1939) (Ford)

Gawsworth, John (ps. T. I. F. Armstrong). *Ten Contemporaries: Notes Toward Their Definitive Bibliography* (Joiner and Steele, London, 1933) (Gawsworth)

Hart-Davis, Rupert. *Hugh Walpole, A Biography* (Macmillan, London, 1952) (Hart-Davis)

James, William. *The Principles of Psychology*, 2 vols. (Macmillan, London, 1901) (James)

Kelly's Directory of Berkshire, Buckinghamshire and Oxfordshire (Kelly, London, 1887) (BD)

Kelly's Directory of Kent, Surrey and Sussex (Kelly, London, 1913) (KSSD)

Kelly's Directory of Somersetshire (Kelly, London, 1883) (SomD)

Kidd, Benjamin. *Social Evolution* (Macmillan, London, 1894), (Kidd)

Macmillan, William. *The Reluctant Healer, A Remarkable Autobiography* (Gollancz, London, 1952)

Mizener, Arthur. *The Saddest Story, A Biography of Ford Madox Ford* (The Bodley Head, London, 1972) (Mizener)

Odle, Rose. *Salt of Our Youth* (Wordens of Cornwall, Penzance, 1972 (Odle(B))

Painter, George D. *Marcel Proust*, 2 vols. (Chatto & Windus, London, 1965)

The Post Office London Directory (Kelly, London, 1896–1917) (LD)

The Post Office Directory of Somersetshire (Kelly, London, 1875) (SomD)

Powys, John Cowper. *Dorothy M. Richardson* (Joiner and Steele, London, 1931) (Powys(A))

Powys, John Cowper. *Autobiography* (John Lane The Bodley Head, London, 1934) (Powys(B))

Report of the British Association for the Advancement of Science (Murray, London, 1869–1916) (RBA)

Wedgwood, C. V. *The Last of the Radicals, Josiah Wedgwood M.P.* (Cape, London, 1951)

Wedgwood, J. C. *Memoirs of a Fighting Life* (Hutchinson, London, 1940) (Wedgwood)

Wells, A. C. *The Book of Catherine Wells* (Chatto & Windus, London, 1928)

Wells, H. G. *Experiment in Autobiography*, 2 vols. (Gollancz and The Cresset Press, London, 1934) (Wells)

Wilkinson, Louis U. (ed.). *The Letters of John Cowper Powys to Louis Wilkinson 1935–1956* (Macdonald, London, 1958)

Woolf, Virginia. *The Common Reader (I)* (The Hogarth Press, London, 1925) (Woolf(A))

Woolf, Virginia. *A Writer's Diary* (The Hogarth Press, London, 1953) (Woolf(B))

B   Newspapers and Periodicals

Anonymous Review of *Pointed Roofs*. *The Times Literary Supplement*, 23 sep. 1915, 323 (TLS(A))

Anonymous Review of *Pointed Roofs*. 'An Original Book', *The Saturday Review*, 16 oct. 1915, Literary Supplement, vi, viii (SR(A))

Anonymous Review of *Backwater*. 'Backwater', *The Times Literary Supplement*, 22 july 1916, 358 (TLS(B))

Anonymous Review of *Honeycomb*. 'Honeycomb', *The Times Literary Supplement*, 18 oct. 1917, 507 (TLS(C))

Anonymous Review of *Honeycomb*. 'According to Miriam', *The Saturday Review*, 24 nov. 1917, 422 (SR(B))

Anonymous Review of *The Tunnel*. 'The Tunnel', *The Times Literary Supplement*, 13 feb. 1919, 81 (TLS(D)).

Anonymous Review of *The Tunnel*. *The Spectator*, 15 mar. 1919, 330–331 (Spectator(A))

Anonymous Review of *Interim*. 'Interim', *The Times Literary Supplement*, 18 dec. 1919, 766 (TLS(E))

Anonymous Review of *Deadlock*. 'Miss Richardson's New Novel', *The Spectator*, 26 mar. 1921, 403 (Spectator(B))

Anonymous Review of *Revolving Lights*. 'Proust, Joyce and Miss Richardson', *The Spectator*, 30 june 1923, 1084–1085 (Spectator(C))

Anonymous Review of *Pilgrimage*. 'Dorothy Richardson', *The Times Literary Supplement*, 17 dec. 1938, 779 (TLS(F))

Chevalley, Abel. 'Les Lettres Anglaises', *Vient de Paraître* (Paris), jan. 1928, 55–56 (Chevalley)

Glikin, Gloria. 'The "I" and the "She" ', *Adam*, 1966, 41–44 (Glikin(B))

Gregory, Horace. 'An Adventure in Self-Discovery', *Adam*, 1966, 45–47

The Gypsy, No. 2, may 1916 (The Gypsy Press, 8 & 9 St. James's Market, London S.W.) (Gypsy)

Hyde, Lawrence. 'The Work of Dorothy M. Richardson', *Adelphi*, nov. 1924, 508–517

Lawrence, D. H. 'Surgery for the Novel—or a Bomb', *Inernational Book Review*, apr. 1923 (Lawrence)

Morgan, Louise. 'How Writers Work: Dorothy Richardson', *Everyman*, 22 oct. 1931, 395–396, 400 (Morgan)

Sinclair, Frederick. 'A Poet's World in Woburn Walk', *St. Pancras Journal*, dec. 1948, 124–127

Sinclair, May. 'The Novels of Dorothy Richardson', *The Egoist*, apr. 1918, 57–59 (Sinclair)

Staley, Thomas. 'A Strange Anachronism', *Adam*, 1966, 48–50

The Times (London), 30 nov. 1895, 7 (Times(B))

The Times (London), 30 aug. 1917, 7 (Times(C))

West, Geoffrey (ed.). 'The Future of the Novel', *Pall Mall Gazette*, 20 jan. 1921, 7

Woolf, Virginia. 'Romance and the Heart', *Nation and Athenaeum*, 19 may 1923, 229 (Woolf(C))

References to Sources

The page number and first two words of the paragraph are cited. Abbreviations refer back to the Bibliography and Source Material. Volume numbers of published works are given in roman numerals, page numbers in arabic. The abbreviations 'RIO', 'DG', 'PB' and 'PBW', on their own, refer to verbal information supplied by Rose I. Odle, David Grad, Philip Batchelor and P. B. Wadsworth. The abbreviation 'P' refers to *Pilgrimage,* (the J. M. Dent 4-volume edition, 1967) and 'SH' to the records of Somerset House

Chapter 1 Early Life

Page Paragraph
1   Dorothy Richardson . . . SH
    The Richardsons . . . SH
    There was . . . SH ; Data, 14 ; RIO
    Following the . . . Data, 14
2   Charles became . . . Data, 14 ; To PK, 2 aug. 1943
    The first . . . SH ; Som.D.
    To Somerset . . . Som.D ; Data, 15 ; P, 111, 249
    His daughter . . . Odle(A), 27 ; SH
3   Settling into . . . BD
    In 1867 . . . SH ; Data, 14 ; BD ; DMR(D)
    A second . . . SH ; BD ; RBA
4   On 17 May . . . Odle(B), 27
    On 13 January . . . SH ; Data, 14
    Disposing of . . . Data, 15, 17 ; RBA
    Dorothy's first . . . Beginnings, 195 ; Data, 15
5   At five . . . Data, 15 ; To HS, 18 oct. 1952 ; To JCP, 31 March 1939
    The atmosphere . . . To PK, 22 aug. 1943
    The four . . . To JCP, 22 july 1941 ; RIO ; To PK, 8 feb. 1941
6   But when . . . Data, 15
    Dorothy, attached . . . Data, 15 ; RBA ; Beginnings, 196
    Dorothy and . . . SH ; Data, 15 ; DMR(E), 606–609
7   In 1883 . . . Data, 15

Page Paragraph
From the . . . Data, 15
But the . . . Data, 15
Dorothy, wilful . . . Data, 16 ; To JCP, 22 july 1941
8   Dorothy and . . . To JCP, 22 july 1941 ; To PK, 28
aug. 1943
In fact . . . To PK, 28 aug. 1943
Charles's tolerance . . . P,II, 102 ; Odle(A), 28 ; To
JCP, 22 feb. 1939
9   Even in . . . DMR to LM, 5 oct. 1931 ; DMR(G),
47,100
Miss Harriet . . . Data, 16–17 ; LD
Amy was . . . Wells, II, 362 *et seq.* ;P,11,89,112–113,
202 ;
To JCP, 15 dec. 1929
10   She was . . . VG(3) to RIO
She cared . . . DMR (F), 39–40 ; Data, 15
Dorothy was . . . Data, 18 ; To PK, 9 june 1943
Of these . . . To PK, 9 june 1943
11   Dorothy was . . . Odle(A), 27 ; To JCP, 19 dec. 1935
At home . . . Data, 16 ; DMR(E), 606–609 ; To HS,
26 jan. 1949
At a . . . To HS, 3 june 1951
At this . . . Data, 16–17
However, appearances . . . To PK, 22 aug. 1943
12   But soon . . . Data, 17
Then for . . . Data, 17 ; P, I, 425
Even in . . . Data, 17 ; P, I, 203
Nothing was . . . Data, 17 ; To PK, 30 aug. 1951
She went . . . Data, 17 ; Odle(A), 29
13   On a . . . Beginnings, 197 ; Data, 15–16
Charles travelled . . . P, I, 118 *et al.*
Dorothy's extremely . . . P, I, 195 ; P, II, 97 ; To
EBCJ, aug. 1923 ; To JCP, 25 oct. 1942 ; Data, 15
14   Dorothy was . . . P,I, 425
She would . . . Beginnings, 197 ; Data, 17
The Misses . . . To PK, 31 may 1936 ; LD ; To JCP,
nov. 1936 ; P, I, 195
15   It soon . . . To JCP, nov. 1936

Page Paragraph

Page Paragraph
24   Unitarianism interested . . . P,III, 233 ; To BE, 9 jan.
      1950 ; To JCP, 14 jan. 1935 ; To Mrs. JA, 1 nov. 1948
      Meanwhile she . . . DG ; VG(7) to RIO
      He and . . . To JCP, 29 oct. 1944
      They read . . . Data, 18 ; P,III, 140–141
25   Her critical . . . DMR(J)
      She and . . . To HS, 31 may 1949
      Her prettiness . . . VG(3) to RIO
      She liked . . . P,III, 113
      His Russian . . . P,III, 240
26   With Badcock . . . Data, 18 ; To PK, 31 may 1936
      She needed . . . Data, 19 ; P,II, 336
      One weekend . . . RIO ; P,IV, 487
      But Benjamin . . . To DG (undated) ; P,III, 151
27   Dorothy was . . . Data, 18 ; to HS, 11 mar. 1950
      She and . . . VG(6) to RIO ; To JCP (undated)
      Daniel and . . . To PK, 21 Feb. 1944
      Dorothy, involved . . . Data, 18 ; DMR(L) ; P,II,
      204–210
28   There was . . . To PK, 20 apr. 1949
      She had . . . PBW ; To RIO, 25 dec. 1950 ; VG(3) to
      RIO
      Benjamin Grad . . . To PK, aug. 1936
      She and . . . DG ; To HS (undated)
29   However, she . . . P,II, 262 ; Data, 18
      But something . . . VG(7) to RIO
      The revelation . . . RIO
      Benjamin loved . . . RIO ; DMR(K)
      Intellectually too . . . To HS (undated)
30   From translation . . . To RIO, 1952
      Always in . . . P, III, 20
      She finally . . . Data, 19
      From time . . . To PK, 21 feb. 1944 ; PB
      Someone else . . . RIO ; DMR(C)
31   She had . . . P,IV, 591 ; To HS, 18 mar. 1950 ; To
      DG, 2 june 1948 ; P,IV, 423
      Receiving the . . . Wells, I, 362 *et seq*
      The two . . . Wells, I, 362 *et seq.*

Page Paragraph
32   Jane also . . . Wells, I, 362 *et seq.*
      Jane's husband . . . Wells, I, 362 *et seq.*
      Wells and . . . Wells, II, 557
      Physically, Dorothy . . . DMR(R)
      He talked . . . Wells, I, 67–68 *et al.*
33   Like Dorothy . . . Wells, II, 540, 601 *et al.* ; Wells, I,
      223
      He loved . . . To HS, apr. 1950 ; Kidd 97 *et seq.*
      It was . . . To HS, 30 oct. 1946 ; To JCP, 25 oct.
      1945 ; To JCP, 1 nov. 1945 ; To DG, july 1948
      According to . . . Wells, II, 469 ; Wells, II, 656 *et seq.*
34   His ideals . . . Wells, II, 435 *et al.* ; Wells, I, 184
      His ideas . . . Wells, II, 436 *et al.* ; Wells, II, 430,
      435 ; To HS, april 1950
      In these . . . Dickson, 84
35   In 1898 . . . Wells, II, 581 *et seq.*, 638
      Dorothy was . . . P,II, 409
      So his . . . Wells, II, 483
      Dorothy had . . . To HS, 31 july 1947 ; To HS, 26
      nov. 1947
36   However, he . . . VG(5) to RIO
      She took . . . To PK, 25 jan. 1944
      Her visits . . . To PK, 16 june 1948
      In 1903 . . . Wells, II, 660–661 *et al.*
      He returned . . . Dickson, 125 ; Brome(A), 30 ; To
      PK, 24 apr. 1937
37   Miss Moffatt . . . VG(5) to RIO
      Dorothy liked . . . VG(5) to RIO
      Dorothy liked her . . . VG(5) to RIO
      They found . . . To JCP, ll june 1935
38   A few . . . DMR(H), 60–66 ; LD
    . The rooms . . . DMR(H), 60–66
      Harder for . . . VG(5) to RIO ; DMR(H), 60–66
39   In 16 Woburn . . . DMR(H), 60–66
      Walking home . . . DMR(H), 60–66
      Now with . . . P,IV, 194
      Charles Daniel . . . DMR(M), 259–263 ; P,III, 369
40   She wrote . . . Data, 19

Page Paragraph

    Meanwhile her ... Dickson, 129 *et al.*; Wells, II, 661–662 ; Wells, I, 255

    His love ... DMR(R)

41   In her ... To HS, 1 feb. 1951 ; Data, 19

    At the ... Beginnings, 197 ; VG(3) to RIO ; DG

42   There were ... DG

    Before settling ... To PK, 27 may 1946 ; To PK, 30 nov. 1949 ; VG(2) to RIO ; VG(3) to RIO

    Having told ... VG(1) to RIO ; VG(2) to RIO ; VG(3) to RIO

    Her feelings ... VG(1) to RIO ; VG(2) to RIO ; VG(3) to RIO

    Wherever she ... VG(5) to RIO

43   Veronica had ... DG ; Data, 19 ; To PK, sep. 1928

    In 1903 ... To Mrs. Tomkinson, july 1949 ; To VG (undated) ; VG(1) to RIO

    Dorothy now ... RIO ; To PK, 2 mar. 1933 ; P,III, 261

    Ill at ... Data, 19

44   At home ... VG(5) to RIO

    As Easter ... VG to DMR (undated) ; RIO

    It was ... Wells, II, 463

    In the ... VG to DMR (undated)

45   They spent ... VG(3) to RIO ; DMR to VG (undated) ; To RIO, 5 feb. 1949

    But Veronica ... DG

    But Dorothy ... VG(1) to RIO

    Her writing ... Beginnings, 197

46   Of all ... DG

    Dorothy wondered ... VG(3) to RIO

    Soon after ... VG(3) to RIO

    Veronica and ... VG(7) to RIO

    She herself ... Data, 19

    The house ... SD ; To JA, 30 apr. 1930

47   Miss Penrose ... SD ; MT to RIO, 3 mar. 1970

    Through the ... To JCP, 23 feb. 1939

    Settled in ... DMR(N)

    The elder ... To DG, 2 june 1948 ; To EBCJ,

Page Paragraph
　　25 nov. 1938
　　She interrupted . . . VG(3) to RIO ; To DG, 13 mar.
　　1937
48　Dorothy was . . . To JCP, sep. 1929 ; DMR(J)
　　Adelboden was . . . To EBCJ, nov. 1927
　　With this . . . DMR(J) ; DMR(O)
49　She struggled . . . To BE, 3 aug. 1949
　　Baumann encouraged . . . DMR(J)
　　However, she . . . DMR(J)
　　But how . . . DMR(J)
　　She worked . . . DMR(J) ; To HS, 6 jan. 1950
50　She thought . . . To HS, 26 aug. 1948
　　Nor did . . . To JCP, 15 dec. 1929 ; To HS (undated) ;
　　To JCP (undated)
　　Working at . . . VG(1) to RIO
　　This hostel . . . VG(1) to RIO
　　She looked . . . PBW
51　A Russian . . . To HS, 15 feb. 1951
　　But Olga . . . To HS, 15 feb. 1951
　　In 1912 . . . Morgan
　　The Beresfords . . . Morgan
　　Dorothy was . . . To PK, late summer, 1934 ; Hart-
　　Davis, 90–92
52　Friends thought . . . RIO ; Morgan
　　But if . . . DMR(J)
　　She had . . . Morgan
　　She threw . . . DMR(J)
　　She was . . . Data, 19
53　Perhaps she . . . Morgan
　　With the . . . Morgan
　　The reader . . . DMR(P), 160–162 ; DMR(Q), 188–
　　192
54　Although every . . . PBW ; Data, 18 ; FG to DMR,
　　1 july 1923
　　Dorothy made . . . DMR(K)
　　She worked . . . DMR to EBCJ, 12 may 1921
　　Miriam was . . . VW(C)
55　Dorothy Richardson . . . P,IV, 613, 657

Page Paragraph

The manuscript ... Morgan ; To JCP, oct. 1938, P,I, 10

Kate's family ... PB ; To HS, 3 june 1951

56   *Pointed Roofs* ... SR(A)

The outcome ... TLS(A)

57   It was ... VW(C) ; P,I, 12

However, despite ... To CB, oct. 1917

On returning ... To BE, 10 dec. 1946

58   On the ... To PK, 22 aug. 1943

Still, Dorothy ... To PK, 22 aug. 1943 ; RIO

Dorothy was ... TLS(B) ; To JCP, 8 nov. 1938

59   She lived ... VG(7) to RIO ; PB ; To JCP, 6 july 1938

Early in ... To RIO, 31 oct. 1949

As they ... To RIO, 31 oct. 1949

On a ... Odle(A), 31 ; RIO

60   She seemed ... Data, 18

All she ... To JCP, 1929 ; To DG, 6 feb. 1939

Sometimes, wakeful ... RIO

These were ... To HS, 29 oct. 1949

His younger ... Odle(A), 31–32

61   That first ... To JCP, 15 dec. 1929 ; To PK, 22 aug. 1943

She discovered ... Gypsy, 149

She found ... To JCP, 24 may 1938 ; To HS, 29 oct. 1949 ; To PK, 22 aug. 1943 ; To HS, 10 oct. 1947

62   If Alan ... To HS, 29 oct. 1949 ; To PK, 25 jan. 1944

Rose and ... Odle(A), 32 ; To PK, 25 july 1930

Hurrying had ... RIO

To Rose ... RIO

63   She and ... Odle(B), 81, 95 *et al.*

Samuel Odle ... Odle(B), 99 *et al.*

Rose's mother ... Odle(B), 99 *et al.*

The talk ... RIO

In fact ... Odle(A), 31 ; To JA, 6 oct. 1945 ; VG(3) to RIO

64   Dorothy, who ... To RIO, 27 nov. 1949

Wedgwood wrote ... Wedgwood, 132

Alan occupied ... To JCP, oct. 1938

194

Page Paragraph
65 He also . . . RIO
    After she . . . Odle(A), 30
    By great . . . Odle(A), 30
    In the . . . Odle(A), 30–31
    His occasional . . . Odle(A), 30–31
66 In 1917 . . . Odle(A), 32
    Back at . . . RIO
    Again he . . . RIO
    In Cornwall . . . AO to DMR, 1917; DMR to AO,
    1917; JCP to DMR, 20 jan. 1937
    This surface . . . PB; Odle(A), 29
67 Having promised . . . RIO
    The date . . . Odle(A), 32
    Mr. Odle . . . Odle(B), 108 *et al.*; RIO
    As for . . . To CB, oct. 1917
    The Times . . . TLS(C); SR(B); Spectator(A)
68 In France . . . Chevalley, 55–56
    It occurred . . . To HS, 29 oct. 1949; To HS, 31 may
    1947; Data, 19
69 The day . . . Times(C), 7
    On the . . . SH; To DG, 6 feb. 1939
    In 'risking . . . Data, 19

    Chapter 3 Novel in Progress, 1913–1917
70 *Pointed Roofs* . . . to HS (undated)
    She had . . . To BE, 7 dec. 1948
    The mode . . . To EBCJ, 12 may 1921
71 Her method . . . To HS, feb. 1947
    It was . . . To JCP, 21 dec. 1947; To PK, 14 oct.
    1947
    But in . . . To HS, 18 mar. 1950; To JCP, sep. 1925
72 The first . . . P,I, 15–16
    As for . . . P,I, 15
73 She awakes . . . P,I, 21
    Accompanied by . . . P, I, 28, 33; JCP to DMR, 2 june
    1930
    The account . . . P,I, 52
74 Miriam's first . . . P,I, 57

Page Paragraph
The first ... To HS, 10 oct. 1949
But Alan ... To HS, 29 oct. 1949; DMR(K)
87   So they ... To RIO, 20 mar. 1948; To PK, 19 oct. 1943
But there ... To HS, 29 oct. 1949
Through her ... To PK, nov. 1943; Odle(A), 32; To PK, 25 july 1930; To JCP, 5 aug. 1944
The Grads ... VG(3) to RIO; DG
88   For feminist ... P,I, 464; Data, 17; P,IV, 223
In these ... To JCP, oct. 1938
A sense ... P,IV, 655; Odle(B), 128; Beginnings, 197
She was ... DMR(K); To PK, 16 june 1948
89   But they ... To HS, 1 May 1951
Days like ... To JCP, 19 dec. 1935
Alan was ... To PK, 10 dec. 1930; To PK, 22 aug. 1943
90   His health ... RIO
Her capacity ... PB; DG
She was ... Sinclair; James, 239
The Times ... TLS(D); TLS(E)
91   Dorothy and ... To PK, 28 aug. 1933
Dorothy had ... DG
Just before ... To HS, 18 mar. 1950
92   A few ... To HS, 18 mar. 1950
In the ... To RIO, 26 aug. 1949
Both he ... To PK, 27 apr. 1950
93   Their friends ... To HS, 26 jan. 1949; To PK, sep. 1928
The party ... To RIO, 1949
It was ... Morgan; Data, 19
At an ... RIO
Another friend ... Wadsworth, 40
94   The revolutionary ... To JCP, 22 jan. 1940
The Odles' ... To PK, 17 june 1929; Beginnings, 197
In the ... To HS, 16 feb. 1951; To HS, 26 aug. 1948
95   She and ... To RP (undated)

Page Paragraph

Her sales ... To CB, oct. 1917 ; To CB ; may 1919

However, her ... Ellmann, 517–519

Her American ... Gawsworth, 199–207; FG to DMR, 1 july 1923

96 John Cowper ... JCP to DMR, 19 jan. 1930

Powys resolved ... JCP to DMR, 30 june 1937

She was ... To EBCJ, aug. 1923

97 None the less Sunday ... To JCP, 24 apr. 1940 ; DG ; To HS, 1 apr. 1949

One particular ... Mizener, 196

Not that ... RIO

He and ... Ford, 848

He passed ... EH to DMR, 8 june 1924 ; EH to DMR, 1 oct. 1924

98 They were ... Bryher(A), 23

Bryher and ... To PK, 2 nov. 1943 ; To RIO, 12 oct. 1952 ; Bryher(A), 23

From this ... To RP, jan. 1924

99 The atmosphere ... To JA, jan. 1924

One of ... To JA, jan. 1924

By April ... PBW ; To HS, 1 may 1932

Invited to ... Wadsworth ; PBW

100 Turning up ... PBW

To Wadsworth's ... Wadsworth ; PBW

After he ... To HS, oct. 1949 ; To JA, 1928

101 The latest ... Spectator(B) ; Spectator(C) ; To PK, 14 dec. 1928

Despite this ... To BE, 27 apr. 1945 ; To JCP, 19 dec. 1935

102 It seemed ... To JCP, 24 may 1938 ; JCP to DMR, 23 dec. 1950 ; JCP to DMR, 1 dec. 1933

Chapter 5 Novel in Progress, 1917–1927

103 At this ... P,II, 13, 20

Dorothy's first ... DMR(H), 60–66

With Jan ... P,II, 93, 98

104 Miriam has ... Data, 18 ; P,II, 71–72

After her ... P,II, 76

Page Paragraph

Chapter 8 The Narrowing of the Way

Page Paragraph

One day ... To PK, 21 feb. 1944; VG(6) to RIO; Daniel, 25

Young Daniel ... To PK, 21 feb. 1944; To JCP, 17 jan. 1940

151 Florence Daniel ... To PK, 21 feb. 1944

Alice had ... To PK, 14 june 1941; To PK, 5 oct. 1946

Harry Badcock ... To PK, 5 oct. 1940; To PK, 11 feb. 1935

Instinctively her ... To PK, 1 jan. 1939

Very occasionally ... To JCP, 24 june 1948

152 The Odles' ... To JCP, 1940; To JCP, 24 apr. 1940; To PK, 12 feb. 1943; To RP, 27 dec. 1944

In 1942 ... To JCP, 1944

His son ... DG

153 Veronica was ... To PK, summer, 1948

In 1944 ... To PK, 8 june 1944

Old age ... To RP, 20 feb. 1944; To HS, feb. 1947

She and ... To PK, 21 july 1941; To JA, 1945; To RIO, 1949

Wells also ... Dickson, 310

154 Dorothy was ... To JCP, 5 aug. 1944; To JCP, 1 nov. 1945

The atomic ... To BE, 1 oct. 1945

There was ... To PK, 14 feb. 1943

155 Benjamin Grad ... DG

But presently ... To DG, June (undated); To PK, summer, 1948

Even in ... To BE, 7 dec. 1948; To HS, 31 may 1947

The French ... To JA, 6 oct. 1945; To HS, feb. 1947

156 In old ... To PK, 14 oct. 1947; To BE, 7 jan. 1948

In the ... To PK, 16 june 1948

It saddened ... To LM, 15 oct. 1950

But Alan ... To HS, 31 may 1947

157 Then one ... To LM, 26 mar. 1948

'No one ... To LM, 26 mar. 1948

'The police ... To LM, 26 mar. 1948

INDEX

The first part is general, the second of characters and places in *Pilgrimage*.
Cross-references between the two are in capitals in parentheses.

I

A.B.C., Restaurant, London, 20, 111

Abercorn Place, St. John's Wood, London, 61

Abingdon, Berkshire (BABINGTON), 1, 3–6, 18, 19, 26, 75, 80, 108

Adelboden, Switzerland, 48, 121

A la recherche du temps perdu by Marcel Proust, 56, 71, 166

Albertine Disparue by Marcel Proust, 128

Allinson, Adrian, 61, 174

All Saints' Church, Barnes (ALL SAINTS' CHURCH), 11, 76, 80

Ambassadors, The by Henry James, 50, 119

Anarchism, 22

Andreyev, Leonid Nikolaevich, 113

Anglicans, 2, 110

Anna Karenina by Leo Tolstoy, 112

Arachne Club, London (BELMONT CLUB), 36, 37, 41

Austen, Jane, 50

Austen, John, 99, 126

Avenue, (6) The, Chiswick, London, 16

Ayre, Miss (PERNE, Deborah), 14, 15, 18, 77

Avory, Horace, Q.C. (CORRIE, Felix), 16, 17, 82

Backwater, 58, 77, 95, 98

Badcock, Eva (HANCOCK, Miss), 151

Badcock, G. W., 28

Badcock, John Henry ('Harry') (HANCOCK, Mr.), 19, 22–3, 26–8, 43, 49, 104, 105, 151, 159, 173

Baker, Keziah (BAILEY, Mrs.), 20, 24, 39, 45, 103

Baldwin, Stanley, 152

Balfour Declaration, 64

Baly, Peyton, Sr. (Charles Francis) and Jr. (ORLY, Leyton, Sr. and Jr.), 19, 104, 159

Barnes, Surrey, 7–12, 14–18, 72, 75, 76, 78, 80

Barnet, Hertfordshire, 19

Batchelor, John Arthur (BRODIE, Bennett), 16, 18, 30, 59, 129, 133–4

Batchelor, Philip (BRODIE, William), x, 18, 30, 59, 130, 174, 175, 176, 177

Baumann, Arthur, 48, 49

Beach, Sylvia, 98

Beardsley, Aubrey, 59

Beckenham, Kent, 175

Belgium, 12

Beresford, Beatrice, 51, 56, 57, 66, 93

Beresford, J. D., 51, 55, 66, 70, 94

Berkshire, 1, 2, 104, 108

Bicester, Oxfordshire, 4

Blewbury, Berkshire, 1, 3, 4

Bloomsbury group, 167

Boundary Road, (58), London, 147

Bowen, Elizabeth, 168

Brand by Henrik Ibsen, 111

Brighton, Sussex, 47

British Association for the Advancement of Science (ROYAL INSTITUTION), 2, 4, 6, 8, 11, 73, 104

British Museum, 21, 55, 95, 112, 126

Brontë, Charlotte, Emily and Anne, 58

Bruton Gallery, London, 92, 93

Bryher, 98, 152

Bunyan, John, 49, 171

205

II